CELESTIAL LOVE

A LOVE THAT'S OUT OF THIS WORLD

MOHAMMAD YUSUF

Copyright © Mohammad Yusuf
All Rights Reserved.

This book has been self-published with all reasonable efforts taken to make the material error-free by the author. No part of this book shall be used, reproduced in any manner whatsoever without written permission from the author, except in the case of brief quotations embodied in critical articles and reviews.

The Author of this book is solely responsible and liable for its content including but not limited to the views, representations, descriptions, statements, information, opinions and references ["Content"]. The Content of this book shall not constitute or be construed or deemed to reflect the opinion or expression of the Publisher or Editor. Neither the Publisher nor Editor endorse or approve the Content of this book or guarantee the reliability, accuracy or completeness of the Content published herein and do not make any representations or warranties of any kind, express or implied, including but not limited to the implied warranties of merchantability, fitness for a particular purpose. The Publisher and Editor shall not be liable whatsoever for any errors, omissions, whether such errors or omissions result from negligence, accident, or any other cause or claims for loss or damages of any kind, including without limitation, indirect or consequential loss or damage arising out of use, inability to use, or about the reliability, accuracy or sufficiency of the information contained in this book.

Made with ♥ on the Notion Press Platform
www.notionpress.com

" With every heartbeat, every glance, every sigh,

I know now, we were meant to be, you and I."

Contents

Contents

Contents

Contents

Aurora Butterfly Presents

Preface

"Celestial Love" is not just a collection of poems, but a journey through the vast, boundless expanse of the night sky, where the moon and stars bear witness to an extraordinary love story. This book is my heart laid bare, my tribute to a love that transformed me, from a quiet, one-sided admirer into a man who believes in forever. It is for her, the muse who inspired it all, the force that compelled me to find my voice as a poet.

The journey began with a simple confession, a poem born of longing and hope. Little did I know, that first piece would ignite an entire saga. What began as a solitary, unspoken love slowly blossomed into a story shared under the veil of starlit nights, full of fireflies dancing like dreams and whispers exchanged between the shadows. This book traces that evolution, capturing moments of yearning, revelation, and the kind of love that refuses to be ordinary.

The themes woven throughout "Celestial Love", the moon, stars, the cosmos, and the quiet magic of stargazing are more than just images; they are echoes of shared memories. My girlfriend, my love, is the heartbeat behind this work. Her passion for the night sky, her delight in gazing at the stars with me, is the inspiration for these verses. And her thoughtful gift of a drawing, two figures lost in wonder under a canopy of stars, reminds me of the beauty in our simple moments.

I offer this book to the world as a tribute to her. A testament of devotion that she may not always see but is always there, woven in the spaces between these lines. She may think I don't value her as deeply as I do, but 'Celestial Love' is proof of my unyielding passion and love for her.

As I share this with you all, I am reminded of the words of the poet, William Butler Yeats: "Until it's mad, passionate, and extraordinary, love, it's a waste of your time. There are so many mediocre things in life, and love should not be one of them." I hope that as you read these poems, you too will feel the resonance of that mad, passionate, extraordinary love, the kind that fills the night sky and dances in the fireflies' glow.

With love and deepest gratitude,

Mohammad Yusuf

Acknowledgements

I begin with gratitude to Allah the Almighty, whose mercy and guidance have been my strength throughout this journey. To my parents, my sisters, and my family—your unwavering love and encouragement have been my foundation. To my lucky charm, thank you for your constant support and belief in me. To my readers, your respect and genuine encouragement have been a beacon of light in this endeavor. To those who provided constructive criticism and feedback, your insights helped refine my craft, and I am deeply thankful for your contributions. I also extend my gratitude to everyone involved in bringing the visuals to life, including the design of this book cover, which I created on Canva. Lastly, I dedicate these pages to the words and visuals that inspire me, woven into the fabric of my work, shaping the poetry that follows.

Introduction

"Celestial Love" is not just a collection of poems; it is the tale of an extraordinary love story—a love that transcends the boundaries of the cosmos, transforming from a one-sided longing into a promise of forever. This debut book takes you on a journey through the emotional highs and lows of a boy who, once a non-believer in love, evolves into a passionate lover.

Written in a unique format, "Celestial Love" presents two parallel stories. The first is the imagined, fictional tale of a one-sided lover navigating the many stages of love, while the second is in form of trivias connecting with real world, intertwined with those imagined experiences. Through the accompanying trivia, I bring to light the personal events and real-world connections that shaped the poems, allowing the reader to glimpse both the fictional and the genuine side of my heart. Each poem represents a different stage of love, from the tentative 'Confession' to the grand 'Paper Ring' proposal, tracing the emotional graph of a relationship that fluctuates between joy and heartache, hope and doubt.

The two lead characters in this story are the lover and his girlfriend, set against a backdrop of cosmic imagery, the stars, the moon, fireflies, and butterflies, elements that have always held a special place in my heart. Along with these celestial motifs, there are subtle nods to things I adore, like Pokémon, Batman, and The Lion King, which add personal layers to the narrative.

The theme of this book centers on a love that is truly 'out of this world', set in a cosmos where time and space cannot limit its depth. The poems reflect the "ECG of a relationship," capturing the peaks and valleys of emotions, and showing how love evolves, ebbs, and flows. This extraordinary tale starts with the uncertainty of unrequited love and culminates in a transformative journey toward forever.

The 40 poems in "Celestial Love" outline the different stages of this love from the confession to the final proposal. As the lover's voice echoes through each line, it becomes clear that love, when nurtured, can evolve into something eternal, something that transcends all boundaries. As the story concludes, the words spoken by the lover leave a lasting impact, a love that resonates far beyond the final page, continuing through the stars and into eternity.

A famous Urdu quote that resonates deeply with this journey is:
"Saari Umar Khud Ko Badnaseeb samjhte rahe, phir ek shakhs ne kaha tum mera pehla ishq ho."
(I spent my whole life thinking I was unfortunate, and then one person told me, you are my first love.)

This book is a testament to the transformative power of love, and it is my heartfelt dedication to the one who changed everything for me. To the girl who became my universe—this story is for you.

POV: Me in love.........

1. Confession!

Hey girl, I hope you're listening me,
My heart says you're still missing me,
Time to tell you something fascinating,
Whenever I thought of you, my heartbeat kept on increasing.
Gravity worked differently when I was around you,
I felt lightened yet constantly pulled towards you.
My brain fermented with images of you,
And I got drunk just thinking of you.
You were my magical stardust,
Which made my love stars to glow harder.
I liked when you made effort to look better,
But I loved you even when you don't.
I was the crystal of ice flakes on the grass,
You were the bright sunshine melting me,
Creating spectrum of light in the prism of love.
Your geometry trapped me in your thoughts.
Your hair seems like dandelions dancing by wind,
Your eyes were the ocean where I could swim.
Whenever I was with you, girl I couldn't figure
out whether it was heaven or earth.
I remember your smile brightened up my soul,
But your touch has faded away which I miss more.
I don't know how to tell but even the sea feels lonely when the moon
is not around.
I wrote your name on the sand,

Knowing it will be washed away in the first wave,

But I was damn sure no one could erase your

name from my heart which was bright and bold.

If there was a way to measure love,

I would spend my life to measure mine for you.

All I did is I loved you in the ways the others never could.

I wish time would have stopped and our life had been on loop.

Whenever I whispered your name nth time,

Even the moon smiled and asked, "Are you thinking of her? Again?"

When you stood in my imagination how could I stop myself from

falling in love with you the nth time.

Girl, listen, I am starving for your soul,

But what I get is only your memories.

Please come back, I promise I will be your Sun providing you the light

to shine.

When you left, like a chameleon I adapted myself,

Then I realized I was a color blind.

The ordinary moments we created, made me to believe, the magic is in

ordinary.

You are not here with me,

I know everyone has to walk their path,

And it is yours to make.

But I promise you, you will be in my stories and I want to be in yours.

Trivia For 'Confession'

"Confession" holds a special place in my heart as it was the very first poem in a storyline that would later become a series. When I uploaded it on my blog, I was amazed by the overwhelming response, readers were so captivated that they immediately requested a second part. That was the moment this idea truly began to take shape, and the story of the one-sided lover was born.

An interesting personal tidbit: when I first shared this poem with my friend, who is now my girlfriend, I had no idea that this poem would be the catalyst for something much bigger. As she read the lines, she told me she was falling for me. I think, in some ways, "Confession" played a part in her realizing her feelings for me. So, this poem not only sparked a story but also, unknowingly, played a role in bringing us closer together.

2. The Lost Letter!

Hey girl, I hope you got my confession,

I am still waiting for your answer.

There are still things which I have not told you,

And I think this life is not long enough to describe you those things.

When I saw you last, I was fermented into two parts,

One part weeped for you and other was still high with your fragrance.

The only thing common between two was,

Both seeped into you.

In my dreams, I am living in those places,

Where I dreamt to be with you,

I am not afraid that it's just a dream,

I am afraid because one day this dream will vanish and I will see my surroundings without you.

I have a request for you,

Breathe me in, let me become favorite memory of you,

I want you to remember me whenever you see the rain,

I want you to feel me whenever the breeze touches your body.

You were the most difficult maze I ever entered,

Because I never found a way to come out of you.

Let me tell you a secret honey,

Even I don't want to come out of this maze.

I looked to faces of many,

I stared into the eyes of a few,

And as much as I try finding you in others,

I always failed because there is simply no one replacing you.

You are now a missing piece of me,

That I am searching for, I feel incomplete without you,

I never knew someone could be both the peace and war within me,

You were that person hiding in me.

I already travelled a long way in search of you,

But I don't want to know if I took the wrong turn.

And though I owe you nothing,

But still I give you my everything.

You left me in such a misconception,

That I even doubt my own reflection.

In helping you to find your way,

I eventually lost mine, And that's fine to me,

Because you reached your destination.

Will you forget me, just as waves forget the moon,

When they crash against the shores?

All the colors you hid within you,

Would put a rainbow to shame,

Please open up and shine honey,

The world will be a beautiful place.

You gave me an addiction,

And the drug of my choice is you.

Fall into me again like a setting sun,

As it sink into the open ocean.

I can still smell you in my dreams,

No matter that my dreams are without fragrance.

You were like my sunshine in a linen,

Warm, bright and most importantly burning me

when I looked at you for too long.

Your smile still lightens me up,

Until it reminds me that you are gone.

I should know by now not to look for you but I am already addicted.

The dense clouds and the water droplets on my window,

Every page of my diary, first to last, the dried flower as book mark,

The blue sky, knowing that your favorite color was blue,

Sweetheart, everything reminds me of you.

Indeed our story was a sad one that needed to end,

Because you never knew the fact someone loved you silently.

You are the memory I will never forget and I will never regret loving you,

Because you are in the love house of my heart and that corner of my heart will beat only for you.

Trivia for 'The Lost Letter'

"The Lost Letter" was, in many ways, an accidental masterpiece. It all started under peer pressure, after the first part of the poem was received so well, I felt a need to continue the story. Initially, I was driven by the desire to reach a wider audience and gain more numbers, so I began writing the second part with those goals in mind.

However, as I wrote, something unexpected happened. Instead of focusing solely on popularity, the poem took on a life of its own. The words flowed more deeply, and I found myself caught up in the emotion and meaning behind the poem, rather than just creating content for the sake of views. What I thought would be a simple continuation turned into something much more profound.

When the poem was released, people loved it just as much, if not more, than the first part. It was a beautiful reminder that sometimes, the best creations come not from force or strategy, but from being in the moment and letting inspiration take its course. "The Lost Letter" became a poem I'm incredibly proud of, and I'm grateful that it evolved into something unexpected yet truly special.

3. Heartbeat!

Hey honey, I hope you got my letter,

Let me tell you, my days are still not getting better.

I am having deja vu of the day the first we said hello,

I felt like a lonely planet who got his moon at that moment.

My heart is losing its rhythm of beating,

I think you could be the one who reminds my heart how to beat again.

Even my bones are aching for your healing touch,

I am looking for you with my parched soul because I know you could
cure any thirst in my bone.

My every season is passing without a single sight of you,

Honey, just show up once I wanna seep within your soul.

I think I set my expectations so high that,

I couldn't even see if the grass was any greener on the other side.

Whenever you feel lost darling,

Look at me as your compass who will show you your true north.

I loved you from all my heart and soul,

And even if you don't, just lie and tell me honey that you love me.

I asked you an answer for my confession,

But your lips are sealed, I don't know why?

So, I will make the most beautiful assumption of this world,

I will keep it a secret, like a prayer you have answered.

My eyes always searched for you, even in the butterflies and fireflies,

But the painful truth was you never looked at me.

I always wanted to tell you honey that you are the first and last love of
my life,

But I never did instead I kept quiet.
Once I thought that your love is only cure for me,
But darling I think loving you silently was fault in me.
Take me back to the moment when we were together,
I wanted to hold your hand and stare at you forever.
You fed me with food of friendship,
But I consumed it as fantasy of love.
I had eaten up every non sense story you told me,
And now see, I am infected by a beautiful virus - 'You'.
Your name always brought smile on my face,
Unfortunately honey, I never told you about this.
Your birthdays were like a festival for me,
Because I get a reason to call you,
But its okay honey you wished me late, I will love you still.

I always searched my masterpiece in you, honey,
But now I came to know our one sided love story was a masterpiece
itself.
You gave me reason to write, you made me a poet,
My love, you gave me a version of myself who is at his best.
Pain never felt so good as in the moment our souls collided,
I wanted to consume your every pain through your lips,
I wanted to drink all your grievances through your tears,
But honey I never did because I never told that I loved you like a silent
lover.
If I ripped my heart from my chest and branded it with your name,
You would still fail to see me, you would still walk away.
You were like a queen bee for me among the different clusters of bees,

Saddest thing was, you thought I was like others just after your 'honey'.

In my fantasies, we created memories I kept safe for rainy days,

Folding back the tips of their pages so as to never forget.

Deep down in your body, I found a soul like my own,

I wanted to place my self in your arms and call it my home.

Our story was sad one that needed to end,

Though I will never regret loving you because love is what you seemed to have needed most.

I know you never found love in me,

But my love I found my masterpiece in you.

Here's a note which I wrote for you, just like my confession I never gave it to you-

"Let me take you to the moon,

On the unicorn and butterflies as guards,

Only me and you and the best ever kiss,

Honey, hold me tightly, let me be your Heartbeat."

Trivia for 'Heartbeat'

"Heartbeat" holds a very special place in my heart, not only because it's my personal favorite but also because it's my girlfriend's favorite work of mine. When she first read it, she told me she had tears in her eyes the whole time. The emotion behind the poem truly resonates with her, and that makes it even more meaningful to me.

A memorable line from the poem, "I am infected by a beautiful virus, You" became a phrase my girlfriend quoted often, because it reminded her of a time when she had actually suffered from an infection. It struck a chord with her, and she embraced It as a symbol of how love, much like an infection, can take over you in the most beautiful way.

A few fun details: the word "honey" in the poem serves a dual purpose, it's both a reference to the sweetness of bees' honey and a personal synonym for my girlfriend, something intimate between us. I also mention the moon, butterflies, and fireflies, elements that have become my signature symbols, which you'll see recurring in future poems. The quotes in the last paragraph were written as part of a fantasy scene, inspired by the dreams I hold in my heart.

4. You, Me and Rain!

Hey honey, sorry to disturb you again,

I am seeing your mirage everywhere.

Do you remember the day it rained heavily?

I do because that rain made my heart wet permanently.

It was our first rain together,

Seeing your wet hair like silk being wet in holy water.

Your eyes were much more beautiful than the rainbow.

Watching your face smiling in the rain was my favourite activity,

Sadly you never noticed me, I was in your background which was blurry.

I saw you dancing in the rain and felt like I was watching the most beautiful creation of God,

I was jealous of rain drops as they touched your lips,

But that jealousy vanished after seeing your lips smiling.

Seeing the rain drops on your forehead was a different kinda thing,

Your forehead was a magnet which was attracting me so that I could feel that heavenly vibe.

Sweetheart, I think only the sky knew how I stared at you like an insane,

Only the butterflies knew that I wanted to give you a kind of love,

That expands like the universe and then collapses and envelopes you again in the same love.

That was the time when cupid's arrow pierced my heart,

All I wanted was to hold your hand and make the monsoon my life's best part.

That rainy day was another life, another time,

I wished I was yours and you were mine.

All I wanted was to fall asleep in your arms, the insects and frogs guarding us,

I was yearning for the love that awaited me in your arms.

That soothing smell of soil was suppressed by the fragrance of yours,

That fragrance made me a permanent slave of yours.

It astonished me how could she shine in those dark clouds,

But her pure beauty explained every bit of that beautiful truth.

That rain was complimentary but your beautiful soul was primary.

Seeing you on a rainy day wasn't something new but a kind of homecoming for me.

There I was surrounded by so many beautiful things, but without you I was empty.

I know you are thinking why I am reminding you again,

Because today also it rained but this time I was deprived of your lovely soul.

That day you didn't even see me once,it didn't hurt me but something within me died.

Honey, just show up once, I want to hold your hands in the heavy rain,

And wants to love you like Romeo did to Juliet.

That day is still my favorite day,

It really hurts to call that day my past but its memories give me reason to smile.

My one wish is still unfulfilled, to rest your lips close to mine,

As a seal and claim you for the rest of my life.

That day all the pain that you endured,

Only made your beauty shine through more.

Honey just one more reminder for you,

When you left that day, you took most valuable thing of mine,

Don't worry I will never ask you back, I will not need it now.

That is permanently yours,

Honey, this is to remind you that day it was me, you and the rain,

And you carried my heartbeat with you,

Can you please show up once because my heart is running out of breath and it demands for you.

Trivia for 'You, Me and Rain'

"You, Me, and Rain" was written on a rainy day, which holds a special place in my heart because monsoon is my favorite season. The rain always inspires me, it's soothing and poetic. However, there's a bit of irony here: my girlfriend actually hates the rain! So, this poem became a blend of my love for the monsoon and the way I wanted to share that moment with her, even though we don't always see eye to eye on the weather.

One of the standout lines from this poem, "rest your lips close to mine," quickly became my signature line, showing up in almost all of my love poems, especially the ones I wrote for my girlfriend. It's a line that captures a quiet yet powerful intimacy, one that's become a hallmark of my writing.

There's also a subtle reference to my possessiveness in this poem. When I mention feeling jealous when someone touches her, even if it's just a raindrop, it reflects the depth of my emotions and how fiercely I care for her. This little detail is a nod to my protective side and the passion I feel in our love.

Another interesting tidbit is the subtle reference to 'Romeo and Juliet'. This poem, like the rain, carries a sense of change and growth, both in terms of my writing and the love story I was crafting. It will always be a favorite of mine for all the layers of emotion and personal touches it contains.

5. Trust Me!

Hey girl, I am back again.

What to do I can't refrain myself from your essence.

I hope you would be reading my every note,

And telling your mates about the extraordinary relationship we mould.

Just to remind you of something unspoken and interesting,

You breathed life into me,

And then left me alone suffocating.

You remember, what a mess we made,

Trying to prove we don't need each other,

And you said, "Trust me, we are made for each other!"

Still many untold stories to tell,

Trapped in my own personal hell, waiting for hope to ring the bell,

Lost in a mind that has so much to tell,

Yet pain mutes my yell,

And you said, "Honey, trust me, you are doing well."

Look me in the eyes, you will see the calmness inside,

Look me through my eyes, you will see everything going wild.

Now what else is there we share,

Other than the absence of one another.

Yet you said, "Trust me, there is nothing to bother.

Just open the book of my love life,

Pages of earth, ink of rain,

Stories of falling, over and over again.

I invite you again to lose yourself in me,

Just the way rain seeps into the sea.

But I know again you will walk away by saying,
"Trust me, we will meet some day, I promise."
I think I tried too hard to love you,
But to love you without you was not an easy task at all.
You played with my heart,
Like an artist play with his art.
Still I will look at you same way as I looked for the first time,
And still you will say, "Trust me, our stars are not aligned.
I wanted to paint your portrait on my canvas through my imagination,
But I was afraid that you might not like the colours,
Which you changed quite often.
I saw you holding hands with someone,
Someone who might be perfect in handling your mess,
But not as good as me trusting you like a defeated soldier trust his
queen in a chess.
I wanted to write those poetries on you,
But you never let me to speak,
Till now those words are silent, they only speak when I open my
notebook.
I don't know why I am feeling toxicated and running out of breath,
Maybe because of the poison you fed me with the syrup branded as
"Trust me" on its packet.
It took a long time for me to get that you only played a game with me,
The worst part of this is knowing that all along
I was nothing but a pawn in your game,
And you were the only one who had my heart.
No matter I lost everything in this epic game,
But honey, Trust Me I am eveready to play this again.
But this time trust me, I am not going to trust you again.

Trivia for 'Trust Me'

"Trust Me" stands as the "villain" of my love story series, the one poem that introduces a touch of negativity into an otherwise extraordinary romance. This poem is unique in that it shifts the narrative tone, depicting the lady as the "villain," which is ironic because in all my other poems, she is portrayed as a symbol of love, tenderness, and beauty. Here, however, she takes on a more complex role, her actions create conflict and doubt in the relationship, making it a pivotal moment in the story.

One of the key lines from this poem, "Look me in the eyes, you will see the calmness inside, Look me through my eyes, you will see everything going wild," speaks volumes about the significance of my girlfriend in my life. It reflects how, when she is with me, there is peace and tranquility, her presence brings calmness to my chaotic world. But when she's not there, everything feels like a battle. This line perfectly captures the duality of my emotions and the depth of my attachment to her. It's a reminder that she is the anchor in my life, and without her, everything seems to fall apart.

In many ways, this poem adds depth and complexity to the love story I've been telling. It shows that love isn't always perfect, it has its challenges, its ups and downs, and even the most extraordinary love can experience moments of doubt and conflict. "Trust Me" is the turning point that makes the resolution all the more powerful.

6. The Last Walk!

Hey honey, I am back again,

What to do, you have that karizma from which I cannot refrain.

You remember? We went on a walk under the moonlight,

Maybe you don't but one thing I remember, that night your face was a competitor for the moonlight.

That night my hand felt the warmth of most beautiful hands of yours

Believe me honey, from that night no other hands fit in my hand better than yours.

That night you were quite but your name was constant in my every talks,

The night was darker but you were like a firefly in the dark night.

When I held your hands tightly, you asked what was special that night,

There were millions of stars but among those stars the moon was in my hand that night.

I wanted to walk with you where sunset met the sky that day,

Because there was hope in its dying light that you will be mine one day.

When you looked at me in my eyes, I saw a fire inside me,

And wondered why everything burned down inside me .

That night I noticed that there were many minute parts of you unexplored,

So I wanted to isolate myself in you like Crusoe for the rest of my life, so those parts get explored.

That night we were standing under a tree to take some rest,

I saw your face sparkling due to moonlight, it was beauty at its best.

I wanted that night to be my longest night ever,

I wanted to walk with you on the road of life forever.

That night whenever you touched me, it felt I have always been yours,

As if your arms have always been my home.

I wanted to feel the fragrance of your lips by making them rest on mine,

But a common boy can't feel it as it was a heavenly gift which was sublime.

That night everything was perfect except one thing,

The flowers which I brought for you were stinking.

Also, I failed to find myself in your eyes,

Everything went upside down when you whispered a name and you wanted to be his wife.

Unfortunately that name was not mine as I was just a substitute for your leisure time,

I will never regret loving you,

I will only regret how long I allowed myself to be fooled.

How conveniently you came to me when your romance grew lukewarm,

As if I was the second best or a good backup plan.

I just want to tell I was never here to compete with your memory or someone else,

I was an artist who wanted to make you his masterpiece whom no one can imitate.

I was like a senseless fighter fighting for the love that was never even truly there,

Even though you were not serious, I showed you authentic care.

That night after the walk you went back to your normal life,

But that boy is still there watching the sunset everyday hoping that one day you will gift him a life.

I don't know how you forgot the affection he had for you,

How can you forget him whose definition for true love was you.

No matter what you did but still I will love you forever,

That hand will still remain empty. I will wait under that tree for you forever.

But I will never forgive you for putting the nail in a coffin, which had a name "true love".

Love will no longer exist in your name,there will come a day,

Maybe, we will be two people meeting again for the first time, someday.

Trivia for 'The Last Walk'

"The Last Walk" holds a deep, personal significance in my journey. I wrote this poem during a time when my friend, who is now my girlfriend and I were not speaking to each other and it felt like our friendship, and possibly even our bond, was coming to an end. I was consumed by the feeling of loneliness, believing we would never talk again. But, as life often does, destiny had other plans for us. We eventually found our way back to each other, and now we're tied together forever.

The poem reflects the pain of that moment of separation, but also hints at the hope and possibility of reconciliation. There's an interesting wordplay with "dark night" (which also reads as "dark knight"), a subtle nod to my favorite superhero-Batman. It's a personal touch that links my love for comics to the emotions I was experiencing at the time.

I also wove in a reference to Robinson Crusoe, drawing from the feeling of isolation I felt during that period, like being stranded on an island, cut off from everything. Despite this, the poem also carries a sense of resilience, just like the character in the novel who ultimately finds his way back to humanity.

Lastly, you'll notice the repetition of my signature line, "rest your lips on mine," which serves as a quiet yet powerful reminder of the intimacy and connection I longed for, even in the midst of our silence.

7. Beyond the Heartache!

Hey girl, look I am back,

One last time, here we go again.

I hope you missed me, well, am I right?

Nah, I don't think so.

Are you trying to erase our memories? I think so.

I want to take you on the most beautiful ride through my words one
last time,

Trust me, it will be the memories for your lifetime.

They called me a storyteller,

And I wrote the stories your eyes told me.

They called me a dreamer,

I dreamt about what love would feel like with my skin in your hand.

They called me a maniac,

Because I saw your side which no one else did.

I was the bullet left idle in your gun,

With just one slip of the trigger and there's no looking back.

Truth doesn't always set us free, my lips confessed my love for you,

And I was imprisoned by your absence.

Yes, I lost the game of love with you,

Your love came at a price I couldn't afford.

I still see your colourful presence in dreams,

In front of that glimpse even the rainbow seemed black and white.

Since I lost you, I am not the same person you left,

I manifested tales of Bruce Wayne and you became my Rachel.

In our stories we were like parallel lines, close but never met.

Just wanted to remind you that people come and go but love remains,
Sometimes beautiful and sometimes a beautiful ache but love remains.
The spark between us would have created an entire universe,
But we decided to be planets in different orbits.
I wanted to know how you smiled when I was not there,
I couldn't help myself but picture a life,
Cuddling under the moon with your favourite cake,
Fighting over who gets the last slice.
They said you had a cold heart,
Is that why you burnt mine just to keep yours warm?
I wish there wasn't so much of you left behind in me,
Your every leftover piece is reviving the demon in me.
I still feel you found me in places, I had yet to find myself.
Very few souls feel like home and you were one of them,
And now I don't have access to that home anymore.
I fell in love and then fell apart but falling apart doesn't seem as bad,
When you are the one helping me to pick up the pieces.
I sabotaged my light so that I can make you shine harder,
After that I was left alone in the dark corner.
Truth doesn't always set us free, my lips confessed my love for you,
And now I am imprisoned by your absence.
I will never be what you want me to be,
So stop trying to fit me into that convoluted little box of yours.
My problem was I kept searching for forever,
In places that led to nowhere.
I stood like a tall tree, my leaves are now falling and I am changing,
I was not meant to stay the same.
Consider what a shadow is like without its host,
And now you can imagine how lost I was without you.

If it's ever your aim to hurt me, don't worry I break my own heart with
its expectations.
I kept losing sight of what could heal me,
Because I was constantly chasing after you.
We built bridges only to burn them and then
I wonder why we feel so lost and far from home.
You never left behind any explanations for your affections,
I was always left to wonder what the hell we even were .
I am glad I was able to keep your idle affection warm,
While you waited for greener grass to graze on.
I wish I could steal the Doraemon's anywhere door,
So I can silently stalk you sometimes.
Please, don't come knocking on the door to my heart,
Love doesn't live here anymore.
There are questions in my eyes, you desperately need to answer.
My skin is a blank page to write your confessions,
Carve those sons into me and we will burn once it's over.
I only wanted you to love me with all my flaws,
I came beautifully packed with imperfections.
Now I am waiting for someone to wrap me in new love,
Because I have forgotten what it feels like.
I wish one day you will wish you had looked into my eyes,
But they will be somewhere watching butterflies, first rain and fireflies
at night.

Trivia for 'Beyond the Heartache'

"Beyond the Heartache" was originally titled "Move On" and was meant to be the final poem in this love story. It was written during a difficult time, as a way to cope with heartbreak and separation, a theme I hadn't originally planned to include in this storyline. At the time, I thought it would mark the end of the journey, but life, and love, had other plans. The reference of Bruce Wayne and Rachel is the reference of scene from The *Dark Knight* when Rachel chose Harvey Dent over Bruce Wayne.

Interestingly, there was a sweet little feud between me and my girlfriend about the title and the direction of the poem. She didn't want me to end the story so abruptly and was resistant to the idea of closure. She even had her own suggestion for the title, but we couldn't agree. In the end, I decided to go with "Beyond the Heartache", as it reflected the idea that love, no matter how painful, is always a part of something bigger-a journey that doesn't truly end, even after hardship. This poem became a bridge between pain and hope, and though it was meant to be the end, it wasn't. It was never meant to be the conclusion, and in many ways, it set the stage for the next chapter of the story.

8. I Love You!

You once asked me if I could stop communicating with you due to the challenges we face.

But your eyes, they spoke a different truth, one that contradicted your words.

It was as if either you or your eyes were hiding something.

Despite the obstacles, there is a quiet healing power in your touch, a comforting presence I cannot fully explain, but one I feel deeply.

In the spaces where wounds go unseen, your touch mends in ways words never could.

I fell in love with the little things about you,

Like sound of your laughter and the way your smile forms.

And listened to you intently, intrigued by your stories of fear, strength and grace,

About being lost in this world and finding my heart in the middle of a storm.

You are far yet so close to my soul,

For, I have a home for you in my heart from the very beginning,

So, you will stay, grow old and be buried with me.

I'm captivated by the scent lingering at your neck,

Just beneath your ear, where your hairline meets the skin.

In that place, I could breathe you in forever.

And when I love you, it feels like lost in my own poetries,

The warmth in winter's night, and the fragrance of roses dancing in the air.

I never said you look nice, you look like a masterpiece,

And a masterpiece is not supposed to look nice,
It is supposed to make you feel something and that feeling is life for me.
I want my hands to not only hold you, but also care for you,
I want my hands to touch you, support you and catch you.
My hands need to work for you, I want my hands to help you,
To give to you , to pray for you.
I want all my body parts to love you like a maniac.
I can die for you baby, and if you'd ask for my heart,
I'd carve it out of my chest and place it in front of you.
I'd write our memories in handwritten letters, drown myself in ink for you.
Will fill my walls with paintings of you because all my eyes see is you.
I'd shatter myself a million times for you,
And if you show me your worst parts, I'd fall in love with them too.
I could spend rest of forever with you,
And wouldn't be enough time to finish everything I have planned for you.
And if you still ask will I be patient in every situation,
I will burn myself and you preserve the remains see me lying patiently.
Don't be afraid my baby, whatever may be the difficulties,
My presence will be constant making you smile again and again,
Your love is here to marry you, claim you with a kiss,
Whenever you will get anxious, you will have my warmest hug.
And if I have choice between breathing and loving you,
I'd whisper 'I love you' with my last breath.

• 43 •

Trivia for 'I Love You'

This poem represents a pivotal moment in the evolving love story of the one sided lover. It marks the transition from a one-sided, uncertain love to an extraordinary, deep connection, serving as a bridge to a new chapter of mutual commitment. In the narrative of the poem, the lover directly addresses his partner's doubts, particularly a moment when she questioned whether he would stay with her. This poem is his powerful response, a statement of unwavering dedication: "I am here to stay." It is his first direct proposal in this storyline, solidifying the future of this relationship.

"I'm captivated by the scent lingering at your neck, Just beneath your ear, where your hairline meets the skin. In that place, I could breathe you forever." This line is inspired by the iconic romantic scenes of Bollywood legend Shah Rukh Khan, known for his portrayal of intense, passionate love. The imagery of the scent lingering at the neck and beneath the ear evokes a deep sense of intimacy and physical connection, a theme often explored in Shah Rukh's films. It captures the delicate and powerful moments of closeness in love, where the senses intertwine, and every touch, every breath, feels eternal.

9. A Romance So Sweet!

A romance so sweet, a tale of two hearts,

A love that endures, never fading or falling apart.

We walk through life, side by side,

Exploring, learning, and with each other, we confide.

We share laughter, we share hugs, we share tender kisses,

The joy of our love is more than enough, a boundless bliss.

With every passing day, our story grows more bright,

Carrying our love, in every step, every light.

Our time together is nothing short of divine,

Our hearts forever intertwined.

We're connected in ways no eyes can see,

Our love will forever be, just you and me.

My love for you deepens with each passing day,

A devotion that is here to stay.

Your eyes, like stars, shine in the night,

Your beauty calms me, filling me with light.

Your touch is gentle, a soothing breeze,

And with every kiss, my heart skips with ease.

The tenderness in your gaze, the love that it speaks,

Makes me feel cherished, fulfilled, and complete.

Your embrace is a comfort I'll never forget,

A love so pure, I never regret.

I feel the depth of this connection we share,

Blessed by the warmth of your love and care.

At times when life brings me down and I'm filled with despair,

I close my eyes and feel your presence there.

You are to me, like coffee in the morning,

A warm shower on a cold winter's dawning.

You're a deep breath when fear clouds my mind,

And when I need you, you're always right on time.

You are the sunshine that brightens my day,

The moonlight that guides me when I've lost my way.

When the moon is full and the night is near,

I hold you close, keeping you near.

How else can I confess my endless love?

I've bowed in 'Sajda,' thanking the heavens above.

For you are my treasure, precious and true,

A woman whose beauty I could never construe.

Your love is a blessing, beyond words to convey,

A wondrous gift, lighting my way.

Each day with you is a gift I embrace,

I could spend an eternity lost in your face.

I live only to see your happiness grow,

For you, my love, I'll give you all I know.

Please take my hand, my heart, my soul,

I long to spend my life with you, to make us whole.

You are my dream come true, my guiding star,

We'll never be apart, no matter how far.

I give you all my heart, for you make me a better man,

For your happiness, I'll do all I can.

Trivia For 'A Romance So Sweet'

This poem is a heartfelt exploration of the deeper dimensions of romance, where love is not only about physical intimacy but also about respect, care, and the profound joy of making your partner happy. In this poem, I wanted to convey that true romance isn't just about grand gestures or passionate moments, but also about the quiet, everyday acts of love that show respect and devotion. The central theme here is that romance is built on mutual understanding and a genuine desire to bring happiness to the one you love.

The inspiration behind this poem came from a conversation I had with my girlfriend, where she expressed her struggle with expressing her feelings. Her words sparked something in me, and this poem became my response, a promise to show her how I would love and romance her, not through words alone, but through actions, through attention, and through deep emotional connection.

One of the most significant elements in this poem is the recurring theme of the moon and the cosmos, which I've used throughout my writings as metaphors for love and longing. The moon has always represented mystery, beauty, and connection in my poetry, and the stars have symbolized the constant, guiding light of love. However, in "A Romance So Sweet", I took a new direction: for the first time, I compared my girlfriend to the 'sun', rather than the moon. The sun here represents positivity, warmth, and life, the source of all energy and joy. It signifies the way she brightens my world and the uplifting force she brings into my life.

10. Kiss Me!

Your lips, when wet and red with wild desire, ignite a flame.

Your eyes, ablaze with passionate fire, leave me entranced.

Your arms, a warm embrace, encircle me, a sweet refrain.

Your hair, a silken touch, upon my cheek, a gentle rain.

So kiss me, sweet, with lips that taste of mutton's savory grace,

And whisper low, with voice both blurred and slow, "You're mine."

Hold me close, beneath the pale stars' watchful gaze,

And let us live this moment, a love divine.

Kiss me in the morning, when the sun first greets the day,

And hold me tight, delaying the world's insistent sway.

"I love you," whisper, then again, and softly, low,

On forehead, nose, and chin, let gentle kisses flow.

Repeat this sweet refrain, an endless, blissful show.

Awaken me with kisses, let your lips ignite my own,

And let us stay forever, in this blissful, dream-spun zone.

I'll cherish every moment, slow and then with wild delight,

Fulfilling all the fantasies that dance within your sight.

Your kiss, a thrilling ride, ascends to starry heights,

A moonbeam's dance, a rocket's swift, celestial flight.

A thunderbolt, it strikes, my heart with sudden grace,

My senses reeling, lost in this ecstatic space.

On angel's wings, your kiss transports me, light and free,

Above the golden meadows, the silver, rushing sea.

A love song, wordless, yet its melody I hear,

A symphony of passion, only in this heart so dear.

Your kiss, a paradise, a heaven of delight,

Let us forever kiss beneath the starry, moonlit night.

I feel your warmth, a rising tide, as sunlight fills the room.

Your hands dispel the shadows, banishing the gloom.

I curl, a silken crescent, knees drawn to my chest,

Imagining the wonders that you do the very best.

Whisper words of truth, let your heart's true feelings gleam,

Your legs, a silken belt, encircling my waist's sweet dream.

You wear me like a favorite shirt, a shade of blue,

A comfort and a passion, forever fresh and new.

Beneath the moonlit sky, a blanket of stars above,

I lie with you, in a far-off, enchanted grove.

A hush descends, only my breath, a gentle, rhythmic sound,

With you so near, my senses lost, no solace to be found.

Your touch, a silken tether, binds my soul to yours,

Lost in your presence, forevermore.

Your kiss upon my neck, a sweet and fiery brand,

My senses captivated, yearning for your command.

As you enter, a smile, a silent, knowing grace,

You pull my hair, I float on air, in this ecstatic space.

Underneath the moonlit sky, beneath a blanket of stars,

I am yours, wherever you are.

Trivia for 'Kiss Me'

This poem, "Kiss Me," is an intimate and sensuous portrayal of an extraordinary kiss that symbolizes deep connection and unbridled passion. The whole collection in this storyline is imagery but in this particular piece, the imagery stands out as it holds personal significance and represents the most cherished aspects of my imagination.

The poem is imbued with a sense of intimacy balanced by deep respect, illustrating that true love is not just about physical connection, but also about honor and reverence for the partner. The playful reference to mutton, a nod to the my girlfriend's favorite food, adds a touch of light-heartedness and personal charm to the piece. This detail is a testament to how I weaves real-life elements into poetry, making the experience all the more relatable and authentic. Additionally, the poem subtly incorporates the girlfriend's favorite color, blue, through metaphors that evoke comfort, passion, and familiarity. The use of imagery in "Kiss Me" goes beyond the typical, capturing the essence of a kiss as an act of devotion and celebration, all while painting a dreamlike landscape that readers can immerse themselves in.

11. A Love That Was Always There!

I'm writing this for a special woman, so rare,

Who holds my heart, my love, my every care.

Dreams of holding you in my arms so tight,

If loving you is wrong, then I don't want to be right.

I dream of the sweetness of your tender kiss,

For you are the reason for my greatest bliss.

Words fall short of what I feel for you,

Through every moment, old and new.

You mean more to me than words can say,

My love for you grows stronger every day.

Every day, I thank the stars above,

That you are mine, my endless love.

I loved you before the world began,

You are the one I choose, my heart's only plan.

To hold your hand, to cherish you,

I love you now and forever, unwavering and true.

Believe me when I say these words with grace:

The love we share is a rare embrace.

Two souls bound, forever meant to be,

You are my soulmate, my friend, my queen.

There is no one else, no one I'd choose,

For you are the light, the love I never lose.

You are the most beautiful I have ever seen,

With eyes that sparkle, so deep and serene,

That sweet smile, that perfect form,
A masterpiece beyond any norm.
Unique and flawless, you are my art,
A vision that captures my heart.
You are my one and only, my highest prize,
I want to be with you, night and sunrise.
To feel your heartbeat, to touch your skin,
To whisper, to hold you, let the night begin.
I want you close, forever near,
With you, there is nothing to fear.
I will love you for all of my days,
My love is steadfast, in so many ways.
Pure, honest, and true, nothing can sever,
No force can stop this love, now or ever.
No distance can part us, no time can erase,
Our bond is eternal, our love a constant embrace.
One day, we'll be together, not just for moments, but for life,
Living side by side, husband and wife.
You are the only one I'll ever call family,
You are my everything, my all, my destiny.
My best friend, my joy, my heart's delight,
You are my love, my life, my light.

Trivia for 'A Love That was Always There'

This poem was written to celebrate a love that has always been there, growing silently and beautifully over time. It tells the story of how a deep friendship slowly evolved into something more extraordinary, true, lasting love. At the heart of this poem is the idea that sometimes the best love stories start with friendship, and that bond serves as the solid foundation for something even more magical. The transition from being good friends to becoming life partners is a journey that's often underestimated, yet it holds the most profound depth and meaning.

As I wrote this, I was reflecting on my own relationship with my girlfriend, how we began as friends, laughing, sharing, and supporting each other through thick and thin, until one day we realized that our bond had blossomed into something deeper than just friendship. This poem honors that friendship, celebrating how it evolved into a love that feels both timeless and irreplaceable.

In every line, I tried to capture the beauty of our connection, how, from the beginning, there was always something special between us that made us more than just friends, even before we recognized it ourselves. It celebrates the rare and extraordinary nature of being not only lovers but also best friends, and how that friendship remains the heart of everything we share today. Writing this poem was my way of honoring the love I found in her, not just as a girlfriend, but as my lifelong companion and soulmate.

12. Forever Sorry, Forever Yours!

Every time I see the pain in your eyes,

A piece of my heart silently dies.

No matter how often or hard I try,

All I seem to do is make you cry.

You risk so much, you give me your heart,

Sharing your hopes, your dreams from the start.

Yet all I do is seem cold and unkind,

Failing to cherish what you've shared of your mind.

My words, they contradict the love I feel,

Thoughts and actions, so far from ideal.

I love you fully, with every part,

Yet act in ways that tear us apart.

I dream of you in the quiet night,

Hanging on every word, every slight.

But all you see is selfish disdain,

In my ignorance, I cause you pain.

I love you deeply, more than I can say,

Yet at times, I push your love away.

I try so hard, but still I fall,

Leaving you alone, while I build the wall.

I scream at myself, so lost in regret,

For risking your love, I can't forget.

I need you more than words can tell,

I pray you'll forgive me, for I am the one who fell.

With every breath, I offer you my soul,

A sincere apology, to make you whole.

No excuses left, no shields to bear,

Just a heart full of love, stripped and laid bare.

Though I falter, though I make mistakes,

Know my love for you, nothing can break.

Every day, I try to do right,

But I still fall short, leaving you in the night.

I'm sorry for the times I was cold,

For the promises I failed to uphold.

I hope, despite the hurt I've caused,

You see my love, and all it's paused.

For all the selfish acts I've done,

For every tear that's come undone,

I beg you now, with all my might,

Forgive me, love, and make things right.

The stars above remind me of your smile,

That I replaced with sorrow for a while.

Now my heart aches, my mind is torn,

For all the hurt, for all I've worn.

Please forgive me, I can't bear to lose,

The one I love, who's paid my dues.

Give me one more chance, I swear I'll change,

To never bring you sadness, or cause you pain.

Trivia for 'Forever Sorry, Forever Yours'

This heartfelt poem, "Forever Sorry, Forever Yours," was written by me as a deeply personal apology to my girlfriend after a moment of disrespect that caused her significant hurt. The poem expresses the raw emotions of regret, guilt, and the sincere desire to mend a fractured relationship. At its core, the poem is a testament to the power of a sincere apology in love, showing that no matter how strong the bond, misunderstandings and mistakes can still occur, but with humility and an open heart, healing is possible.

The poem is part of this collection and storyline because I wanted to convey a powerful message: in relationships, it's crucial to set aside ego and pride. Apologizing when you're wrong is not just an act of humility, but an act of love. It's a reminder that, even in moments of tension and emotional distance, a simple "I'm sorry" can be the key to restoring connection and trust. This poem is an emotional plea to my girlfriend, underscoring the importance of saying sorry in relationships and recognizing that love can always triumph, no matter how far things might fall. "Forever Sorry, Forever Yours" stands as a powerful declaration that love isn't perfect, but it is worth fighting for, especially through honesty, vulnerability, and the courage to apologize.

13. A Love Written In Stars!

Today, I want to share the story of the day I first met you. But if I reveal too much truth, please keep it between us.

Do you remember when I first asked you to meet me, and you said yes without hesitation?

It felt impossible for you to come, but you still agreed.

We were to meet after six days, but we lied to our families to make it happen.

Do you recall I told you to tie your hair up?

My love, my lips didn't tremble once while I lied,

But how do I tell you that those six days of waiting to meet you felt like an eternity?

Every day, I wished time would move faster,

So that moment could arrive, and you'd come to me like the perfect balance of spicy kebabs and fragrant biryani.

You ordered that T-shirt for me with such joy,

And to me, it felt like a child receiving their first toy.

You must remember asking your mother for permission to leave,

And do you remember the look on my face, almost on the verge of tears, waiting for her 'yes'?

It took a little while for your mother to let you come,

How could I explain to her that this peacock had stopped the rain, just for his peahen?

You were frustrated with my persistent questions, asking you to talk to your mom,

But my love, tell me what does a sea do but wait patiently for its shore?

Even now, remembering your face when you finally received your mom's approval, my soul bursts with joy.

How do I tell you that, in that moment, it felt like I had seen the entire sky while standing on earth?

Do you remember that night, the one before we were supposed to meet?

You knew I couldn't sleep because I longed to hold your hand and walk with you to the moon.

That morning still lingers in my heart, because that feeling found a permanent home inside me.

I couldn't believe that God had crafted a day for us to meet.

That morning, I woke up earlier than usual,something felt different in the air.

Even my mother noticed the redness in my eyes.

You probably don't know this, but I spent so much time perfecting my face,

Polishing it as a jeweler would a precious diamond.

I know you were upset when I took longer than expected,

But honestly, I was frozen, just seeing you, so beautifully dressed.

I wore your gift so carefully, like it was the Kohinoor diamond,

And though people stared, I wasn't worried about bad luck, because that black shirt was the most beautiful thing I had.

You left early, and I was delayed,

Perhaps I was the first lover to treat his beloved in this way.

But when I saw you in that pink suit, I felt butterflies flutter in my chest.

With your hair tied up and that radiant smile, I thought I'd seen an angel.

I forgot to ask you, how were you looking into my eyes?

Because all I could see were flashes of lightning in mine.

You kept asking me to look into your eyes,

But my love, you didn't notice how my hands and feet trembled.

How do I explain that I was restless, simply wanting to look at you?

You reached out your hand, and for a moment, I thought of holding it,

But then I hesitated, because if I did, the dream would become real.

Our story was a little backwards, your gaze on me, and me shyly turning away.

My quiet urge to move closer, only to step back in nervousness.

You saw my face when you fed me with your own hands,

And it felt like a lover had finally confessed his heart to his beloved.

I still remember your fragrance from that day, there was something uniquely beautiful about it.

Do you remember asking, "What's that sound?"

My love, that sound was the voice of my heart, speaking only for you.

You were upset when I quickly pulled my hand away from yours,

But my love, I couldn't bear it any longer; I felt like I had won the world.

Do you remember when you sat beside me, and I thought of kissing your lips?

But life needs more than just a reason to live.

When you gently tugged at my cheek and smiled at me,

You probably didn't know, but inside, I was falling apart.

My love, do you know what my favorite moment was that day?

That soft, low music playing, your head on my shoulder, and my heart racing in my chest.

Do you know what my worst moment was that day?

It was watching you leave, not being able to hug you,

Your reluctance to go, and the sun setting behind us.

I still wonder what I should ask Allah for, what I should wish for,

If I could, I would go back to that day and live my entire life in that single moment.

You might be wondering why I'm telling you all of this now,

My love, I know I've troubled you enough, but I'm simply sharing the truth of my heart.

You ask me why I think so much and get upset,

I just want you to be happy, but for some reason, I keep making mistakes.

The truth is, I love you more than anything,

Just as the sun burns for the moon.

I swear, my love, if tears ever fill your eyes because of me,

I'll gather them and turn them into pearls, just for you.

You said you were feeling unwell today and asked me not to write about you,

But my love, I'll fulfill every word I've spoken to you, even if my heartbeat fades.

Do you remember telling your friend, "Falling stars don't exist anymore, wishes don't come true"?

My love, here, take my heart, throw it into the sky, and break it,

Let it shatter so you can make all your wishes come true.

Trivia for 'A Love Written In Stars'

"A Love Written in Stars" is a heartfelt and genuine reflection of first date. The poem captures the true emotions and excitement of that initial meeting, portraying the nervousness and joy that come with meeting someone special for the first time. The simplicity and rawness of the poem mirror the honesty of the feelings involved, making it deeply relatable and intimate for anyone who has experienced the magic of a first date.

The poem contains several personal touches that make it unique to my life. For example, there's a reference to my all-time favorite foods, biryani and kebabs. This small but significant detail adds a layer of warmth and personality to the poem, grounding it in real-life experiences that I cherish. Additionally, the poem humorously references a funny incident from that first date: while the girlfriend showed up on time, I myself was late. This playful moment is captured with lightheartedness, yet it highlights the genuine excitement and sometimes awkwardness of a first meeting. The simplicity of the poem is purposeful. It maintains an unpretentious and raw quality, reflecting my unfiltered emotions. This approach emphasizes the purity of the feelings that arose on that first date, allowing the poem to resonate deeply with anyone who has experienced love in its most innocent and unguarded form. Every word feels personal, and the poem's unrefined beauty adds to the emotional power it holds.

14. Heartbeat 2!

Hey honey, look who's back again,

That lover boy is unstable once more, seeing your mirage.

Baby, do you remember the last time I starved for you?

But this time, I write with the moon by my side-you.

You once asked me what love tastes like,

And I simply pressed my lips to yours, answering with a kiss.

Your love was like starlight, guiding me home,

To the place where my heart was always meant to be.

I wrote poems about our first kiss,

And when that day arrived, you consumed my eager lips,

I lost my breath in your kiss, in your embrace.

No one has ever touched my soul the way you have,

You awakened a part of my heart that now beats only for you.

You once asked me why it took so long to propose,

To call you my queen.

I spent too much time fearing what scared me,

And not enough time embracing what excited me.

But now, I stand before you, ready to shout to the world,

How deeply I loved you, how much I starved for you,

Like the sky, parched during storms, yearning for the color blue.

Baby, I know these days we will not be together physically,

I won't be there physically, but I will love you to the fullest,

Just as you manifested me.

Whenever you feel lonely and cry for me,

I'll be there, in the form of your tears,

Rolling down like diamonds, brushing your lips softly,

Then vanishing as they touch the earth.

When you miss our long walks together,

Jaan, return to that beach and find my footprints,

Waiting to walk beside you again,

Like the rain nourishes the crops, making them bloom.

And when the rain fades, those footprints will be swept away,

Carried by the waves, just as the rain only comes once a year.

When you miss our lingering kisses, sweetheart, don't worry,

I will be there in the cold breeze, kissing your lips softly,

Before vanishing again into the night.

Whenever your hand feels light, starved for my touch,

Hold a dandelion in my field, and feel my presence,

As the wind takes it from your fingers.

When life feels devoid of color,

Look for the butterflies around you;

I will be there, sprinkling magic before disappearing,

Like a burst of love that dances away with them.

Whenever darkness falls upon you,

Catch a firefly, whisper my name,

And let it burn bright until it fades,

A beacon of my love in the night.

When your skin feels dry and pale,

Close your eyes, look to the sky,

I will come to you in the form of rain,

Restoring your glow, making you shine.

When you miss the unexpected snacks I left at your door,

Just look up, my love,

I will be there in the form of a rainbow,

Bringing you the seven most delicious foods in the world.

Whenever you feel gravity weakening,

Look to the moon, my love.

I'll pull you close, just as I did during our first kiss.

When life feels less entertaining,

Watch the movies I recommended,

And feel my presence beside you, whispering,

"Put your head on my shoulder."

Whenever you long for my voice,

Listen to the songs I shared with you,

And hear me whisper our secret code,

"I love you."

When you're angry,

Hold my heart, the one I gave you,

Throw it high, break it,

And let it fall as a shooting star,

Granting your wishes with its fall.

When you feel low,

Place your hand on your chest,

And feel the rhythm of my heartbeat,

The heartbeat I gifted to you.

When you feel lost,

Remember how I once called you my victory,

My queen, my everything.

When you feel cold,

Look at our pictures,

Remember the smiles we shared during our first embrace.

When you miss the poetry I wrote for you,

Look back on the moments we shared,

For those are the very moments I wrote about.

And if ever you wonder how someone could love you this much,

And yet not present physically,

Look at me, baby.

Your love is here in front of you,

Telling you these stories through poetry.

I know sometimes you wonder why we keep our love hidden,

But we both know it's because we found something the world is searching for.

In the past, I ran from you, afraid of the storm,

Until I realized you were the umbrella all along.

Now, my name lives at the tip of your tongue,

A spell that can never be broken.

I used to listen to my mind,

Until I realized that only the heart can decide who to love.

The heart dictates such splendor,

And my heart chose you.

When I see you smile, or roll your eyes,

You shatter every doubt I had about love.

Baby, I hope that every day you look at me,

And see everything you've ever dreamed of.

Your soft lips make me want to tie the knot,

To bind us together, forevermore.

On the road ahead, blowing kisses with you,

I want nothing more than your happiness,

That's my mission.

In these months we've shared,

Has it been heaven or earth?

I can't tell the difference,

Because with you, I feel like I'm in both.

Here's my another note to you, honey:

"Let's sit near the lake, under the moonlight,

Fireflies lighting our way, and butterflies standing guard.

Rest your lips on mine, savoring the nectar,

As I place a paper ring on your finger.

I'll hold you close, our hearts synchronizing,

Becoming one beat.

Come closer, baby, let me be your heartbeat."

Trivia for 'Heartbeat 2'

"Heartbeat 2" is a deeply personal and significant continuation of my earlier work, "Heartbeat." This poem is particularly special to me as it explores the emotional landscape of a love that transcends physical distance. While "Heartbeat" focused on the physical presence of the lover, "Heartbeat 2" delves into the emotional connection between the two when they are apart. The poem offers a tender, heartfelt explanation of how the lover would continue to love and be with his girlfriend even when they are not physically together. It is a beautiful reflection of longing, devotion, and the promise of eternal love.

The foundation of "Heartbeat 2" lies in a line from the previous poem where the girlfriend expresses her belief that "stars don't fall now, and wishes don't come true." This line becomes the emotional anchor for the continuation, transforming into the central theme of how the lover will make her wishes come true, even from a distance. This poem was, in fact, inspired by a long-standing wish of my girlfriend, to write a continuation of "Heartbeat," something she had hoped for and dreamed of for quite some time. Her desire for a deeper connection, expressed through the continuation of the poem, fueled the creation of "Heartbeat 2."

In this poem, the girl is first addressed as "Jaan," which is significant not only because it deepens the intimacy of their relationship, but also because it sets the stage for the next poem in the series, titled "Jaan." The final paragraph of "Heartbeat 2" echoes a note similar to "Heartbeat," tying both poems together and creating a sense of continuity in their love story. Through this poem, I have not only fulfilled my girlfriend's wish but also

expresses how love can transcend distance, becoming an eternal heartbeat
that never fades.

15. Jaaaan!

In the still of dawn's first light,
Where shadows dance and stars take flight,
There's a beauty rare, fierce and true,
A queen with eyes of emerald hue.
Jaan, you move with grace so pure,
A spirit wild, strong and sure.
Your laughter, like a waterfall's song,
A melody where my heart belongs.
Silk-dark hair in waves that fall,
A crown upon your regal call.
Your smile, a sunrise, warm and bright,
Turning the dark to radiant light.
Eyes that shimmer, deep and wise,
A world reflected in your guise.
Your soul, untamed as the forest's might,
A white tiger, fierce in the night.
With each step, the world stands still,
Nature yields to your gentle will.
Paws so soft, yet claws of steel,
A strength that makes the earth feel real.
Jaan, you are the forest's pride,
The ruler of the hidden side.
A creature both delicate and strong,
A paradox that sings my song.
In your presence, time and space collide,

My fears are gone, my heart's my guide.
You are my sanctuary, my guiding flame,
My heart's protector, my eternal claim.
Like in the Golden Compass tale,
Where souls are bound, and hearts prevail,
You are the light in my shadowed night,
My tiger, my spirit, my love, my might.
In the stillness of the midnight air,
Where stars weave stories, beyond compare,
You stand, a vision of strength and grace,
A timeless beauty in a fleeting space.
Your touch, a whisper, soft and kind,
Yet in it, a power undefined.
Like thunder beneath a gentle breeze,
You bring the storms, yet grant me peace.
Through every trial, through every storm,
You are the flame that keeps me warm.
A fire that never fades away,
A love that grows with each new day.
Jaan, you are more than just a name,
You are my soul, my heart's pure flame.
My life, my compass, my reason to be,
You are my everything, my world, my reality.

Trivia For 'Jaaaan'

The poem 'Jaan' is a powerful piece that uses the personification of a white tiger to symbolize the lover's girlfriend, showcasing her qualities of rarity, purity, strength, and wisdom. The white tiger, a creature that is both majestic and fierce, perfectly embodies my view of my partner as an unparalleled presence in my life, majestic, untamed, yet protective and comforting. The poem takes inspiration from 'The Golden Compass', a story in which characters' souls are represented by animal companions called daemons. This connection serves to highlight how my girlfriend is my guiding force, just as the daemons are to their human counterparts. She is described as my "soul" and a part of my very being, illustrating that she is indispensable and deeply interwoven with my life.

The choice of the white tiger is significant, as it embodies duality: soft and gentle yet powerful and strong. This reflects my perception of my girlfriend, who balances kindness with an inner strength that can stand against any challenge. The poem's title, 'Jaan', meaning "life" or "beloved," emphasizes that the girlfriend is not just a partner but his core, the essence that completes and defines him. The imagery of the tiger's soft paws and sharp claws captures the paradox of tenderness and strength, further enhancing the portrayal of our relationship as one filled with both love and an unyielding sense of protection.

Beyond the metaphors, the poem expresses the fundamental idea that the my girlfriend is the center of my world, my sanctuary, and my guiding light. Her presence dispels fear and gives me a sense of purpose, underlining her value and importance. This tribute is not just personal but universal, celebrating how love can be both profound and transformative. Through 'Jaan', I have illustrated that true love is rare and powerful, capable of making life feel complete and meaningful.

16. Fractures And Fusions!

In the garden of hearts, we once grew,
A bloom of petals, vibrant and true.
Soft whispers of green, the scent of spring,
A promise of love, a living thing.
But storms came roaring, wild and fierce,
Dark clouds gathered, lightning pierced.
Our flower, once a radiant hue,
Trembled under skies so gray and blue.
The wind's sharp fingers tore at the seams,
The rain, a torrent, washing dreams.
Petals fell, a fragile cascade,
An aching beauty, now half-made.
In the silence after, where shadows lay,
A broken stem, a heart's decay.
Yet, in the soil, beneath the pain,
A murmur of life, a gentle strain.
Roots reached deep, in search of light,
Sinking, feeling, through the night.
Sunshine returned, warm and kind,
The earth embraced, in a dance so blind.
Drops of dew, like tears in wait,
Sparkled like diamonds, washed in fate.
The whispers of the wind, soft and true,
Brought the scent of love anew.
New petals unfurled, trembling, bright,

A fusion of heart and the morning light.

Colors richer, layered, deep,

Stronger now, a promise to keep.

Each petal told a story, a song of scars,

Of fights that broke, of falling stars.

Yet, here it stood, steadfast, whole,

A testament to the heart and soul.

The rain, once an enemy, now a friend,

Brought nutrients, life to mend.

The sun, the wind, the gentle sway,

A symphony that heals the fray.

Our flower, no longer a single thread,

Was more than before, with colors spread.

Each fracture, now a part of its grace,

A perfect mark in its embrace.

And so, in this garden, we learned the truth,

That love, in its nature, needs the proof.

That even when storms leave us torn,

New beauty blooms, reborn, adorned.

Our love, a flower that's seen the night,

Grows deeper still, in the morning light.

Fractures heal and fusions bind,

A masterpiece, once broken, now defined.

Trivia For 'Fractures And Fusions'

Fractures and Fusions is a poem that uses the personification of a flower to illustrate the struggles and growth within a relationship. The narrative follows the journey of a bloom that faces harsh storms and fierce winds, symbolizing the fights and difficult times that couples often encounter. These trials initially threaten to break the flower, but ultimately, they contribute to its strength and renewal. This theme captures the essence of how conflicts can be integral to building a deeper, more resilient love.

The poem conveys that, while fights and challenges in a relationship can be painful and leave emotional scars, they are also catalysts for growth and transformation. Just as the flower's petals fall and the stem seems broken, the relationship experiences moments of discord and fragility. However, through these experiences, the bond becomes stronger, with new, deeper petals unfurling, each one carrying the weight of past struggles and now richer, more profound in color and meaning. The poem emphasizes that, in love, both pain and beauty coexist and contribute to a stronger foundation.

The poem's narrative aligns with the story of one-sided lover that have endured past difficulties but have reached a point of mutual understanding and health. The fights are no longer destructive but are a part of the dynamic that makes the love more robust and meaningful. The poem suggests that the relationship has evolved from being fragile and fragile to being fortified through its trials.

In real life, this poem has a personal connection. It was inspired by a moment when I wrote a Hindi poem for my girlfriend after a significant fight. 'Fractures and Fusions' represents an evolved and English adaptation of that original poem, illustrating not just a moment of vulnerability but the strength that can come from embracing the full scope of a relationship's journey. Through the flower's symbolic growth, the poem highlights that love, in its truest form, thrives not in the absence of conflict but in the fusion of hearts after facing it.

17. Infinity Forever!

Your love is my home, my sacred space,
A refuge where my heart finds grace.
In your embrace, I've grown so strong,
Your love, my song, where I belong.
With you, I've found my place to be,
A world that's woven just for we.
You are my peace, my calm, my guide,
Forever and always, right by my side.
Your touch is like a summer breeze,
It lifts my soul with gentle ease.
In your warmth, my heart is won,
In your love, my life's begun.
Your flame burns bright, both fierce and pure,
A fire that's endless, forever sure.
With every whisper, every sigh,
You light the stars in my darkened sky.
Your eyes are windows to your soul,
In them, I find my heart made whole.
Your laughter is a melody so sweet,
With you, my love, I feel complete.
Your love, a rain that falls so kind,
Washes my soul, clears my mind.
You soothe the storms, you calm my fears,
You're the song I'll sing through all the years.

You are the sun that warms my day,

In your arms, I lose my way.

When clouds arise, you light my path,

In your love, I find my calm.

Through every trial, through every tear,

I'll love you always, forever near.

My heart, my soul, they both are yours,

With you, my love, I'm always sure.

You are my soulmate, my guiding star,

No matter where we are, you're never far.

In your love, I've found my way,

Forever bound, we'll never sway.

You are my moon, my stars, my light,

My shelter in the darkest night.

Your beauty radiates, both fierce and true,

In every part of me, there's only you.

In your arms, I find my peace,

A world where love will never cease.

Where laughter echoes through the halls,

And joy, in every moment, calls.

With you, my heart beats strong and clear,

A love that wipes away all fear.

In your touch, I find my soul,

With you, my love, I'm finally whole.

Your grace, a dance, so free, so pure,

A beauty that can't be measured, sure.

Every step you take is like a song,

With you, my love, I belong.

Your voice, a symphony so sweet,

Your laughter, an endless heartbeat.
In everything you are and do,
I find my love, forever new.
My love for you is like a rose,
Its bloom, a promise that forever grows.
With every petal, soft and true,
I fall deeper in love with you.
Your smile, a light that warms my heart,
A love so deep, it will never part.
In your eyes, I see our fate,
A love that's pure, and never late.
With every breath, I feel your grace,
Your love shines brightly on my face.
No matter where the road may bend,
Our love will last, it has no end.
Forever bound, heart and soul,
Together, love, we make us whole.
Our journey's just begun, it seems,
A love that lives in endless dreams.
Guide me through the darkest night,
In your love, I find my light.
A love that wraps me warm and tight,
And guides me with a steady might.
Through every storm, through every strife,
You are my compass, you are my life.
In your love, I'll always be,
A part of you, and you of me.
Your touch, my love, is like the sea,
Vast and deep, eternally.

With tides that rise and fall with time,

Your heart beats with a rhythm divine.

A love so pure, so vast, so wide,

With you, I'm whole, with you, I'll glide.

Through oceans deep, through skies above,

My heart beats only for your love.

I've kept some butterflies as our common pet,

And fireflies, a night lamp we won't forget.

You heal my soul, my heart, my mind,

In your love, I'm always fine.

With you, I'll walk till Infinity's door,

In your love, I need no more.

Together, we'll journey through all of time,

A love that's endless, forever sublime.

So here's my vow, my love, my dear,

To cherish you always, forever near.

Through every tear, every laugh, every sigh,

With you, my love, I'll always fly.

For where you are, I will be too,

A heart, a soul, forever true.

In this life, and in the next,

Our love will never, ever be vexed.

For in you, my love, I've found my home,

Wherever we are, together, we roam.

In every universe, in every place,

Our love is constant, our hearts embrace.

And when all else fades into the night,

It's your love, my dear, that's my guiding light.

Trivia For 'Infinity Forever'

'Infinity Forever' is the emotional culmination of a larger narrative arc that begins with 'Fractures and Fusion'. While 'Fractures and Fusion' explores the emotional turbulence of love — the moments of heartache (fractures) and the healing (fusions) that follow, Infinity Forever marks the turning point where these challenges culminate into a promise. It's the moment when love finds its grounding and solidifies into something eternal, unbreakable, and filled with gratitude. In this poem, I have reflected on how, after navigating struggles and pain, the bond with our partner is made stronger, fixing the course of their relationship "forever."

The real-life inspiration behind 'Infinity Forever' stems from a deeply personal moment. Written after my exams, during a time of nervousness and stress, the poem is a heartfelt expression of thanks to my girlfriend. Her nurturing presence, much like that of a mother, helped me navigate through difficult times, and this poem serves as a tribute to her unwavering love. It is a way of saying "thank you" for being the emotional anchor during a moment of uncertainty.

At its core, 'Infinity Forever' is about healing, gratitude, and the promises that solidify love. The poem explores how, after experiencing life's fractures, love and the care we give each other has the power to heal and strengthen. The title itself reflects the timeless nature of the bond, symbolizing a love that transcends time and circumstance. It is a declaration of a love that will continue without end, through all trials and triumphs.

18. You Are The Gift!

Hey honey, look who's back,

Your one-sided lover is here once more.

I've always dreamed of writing for you on your special day,

Though I missed a few chances, I'm here now, on your 20th birthday.

To my incredible girlfriend, on your special day,

I want to express my love in every possible way.

You're the one who fills my world with light,

Happy birthday, my love, my heart's delight.

Your eyes shine with love so true,

On this day, let me shower my love on you.

You brighten my days and warm my soul,

Happy birthday, my love, you make me whole.

You are everything I could ever want, my love so pure,

On this day, my heart is certain, my feelings are sure.

You complete me in ways I can't describe,

Happy birthday, my love, my reason to thrive.

Forever grateful for you, my love so true,

On your birthday, I give my heart to you.

You are the joy that fills my life,

Happy birthday, my love, sealed with a kiss.

A love beyond measure, my heart holds tight,

On your special day, let our love take flight.

You make my world complete, my heartbeat,

Happy birthday, my love, so rare and sweet.

You are my guiding star, my love so bright,

On your birthday, let's embrace the night.

You lead me through every storm and fear,

Happy birthday, my love, I'll always be near.

With you, I'm whole, my love so pure,

On this day, let our love endure.

You are the joy that fills my heart,

Happy birthday, my love, never to be apart.

You inspire me, my love so grand,

On your birthday, let my love expand.

You fuel my dreams, my endless delight,

Happy birthday, my love, with all my might.

Your smile melts my heart, so true,

On your special day, my love I renew.

You bring joy and light, my love sincere,

Happy birthday, my love, forever dear.

Forever in love, together we'll be,

On your special day, let our love run free.

You hold the key to my heart, my soul,

Happy birthday, my love, you make me whole.

Through your eyes, I see love's pure grace,

On your special day, let love's embrace.

You bring magic to my world, my pearl,

Happy birthday, my love, my precious girl.

You're my best friend, my love so deep,

On your special day, my love I keep.

You understand me like no one else,

Happy birthday, my love, I'm forever blessed.

Forever bound in love, my heart is yours,

On your special day, let love pour.

You hold my heart, you're my everything,

Happy birthday, my love, let my heart sing.

A love so deep, a bond so true,

On your birthday, my love will renew.

You make my heart sing in every way,

Happy birthday, my love, today and every day.

In love's perfect rhythm, we dance as one,

On your birthday, let our love shine like the sun.

You make my world complete, my heartbeat,

Happy birthday, my love, you're my ultimate treat.

Here's to forever with you, my love so true,

On your special day, my heart sings for you.

You fill my life with joy and light,

Happy birthday, my love, my guiding light.

Our love, a journey, hand in hand we walk,

On your birthday, let love's melody talk.

You bring me joy, you make life bright,

Happy birthday, my love, my heart's delight.

You're my happily ever after, my colorful butterfly,

You light my path in the dark, my firefly.

You're the unicorn on my best journey through life,

Happy birthday, my darling, my partner, my wife.

We began this journey as friends from class one,

Now, lovers and partners, together as one.

I don't know how I survived those days without you,

For now, my heart beats only when I see you.

You are my peace, my queen, my little baby,
Happy birthday, my love, my lady.

• 94 •

Trivia For 'You Are The Gift'

"You Are The Gift" is a poem I wrote for my girlfriend on her birthday, and it holds a special place in my heart. The poem was meant to be a grand gesture, a celebration of her and the incredible gift she is to my life. In the verses, I painted a picture of how I would celebrate her birthday through my words and poetry. It was my way of showing her that, for me, her special day was like a festival, a celebration of everything she means to me. I wanted to remind her that she is the greatest gift life has given me, and that her presence in my life fills it with joy and beauty.

The imagery in the poem is meant to convey just how deeply a lover can cherish his girlfriend. From the way I describe celebrating her through poetry to the idea that her birthday is more than just another day, it's a day of wonder and celebration, one that I would mark with all the love and adoration I could muster. I wanted to make her feel special, to show her that she is irreplaceable, and that her happiness means the world to me.

However, as life often goes, the reality of the day didn't quite match the poetic dream I had set out to create. Ironically, when I sent her this poem on her birthday, we had just had an argument. I still remember the moment, it was both funny and a bit tragic. Here I was, pouring my heart out in a poem, trying to make her feel like the queen she truly is, and we were in the middle of a disagreement. It was one of those moments where life decides to throw a curveball, and the very thing that was meant to be a symbol of love and peace turned into a reminder of how real relationships are full of ups and downs. Love, after all, isn't about everything being flawless, it's about the moments that make us stronger together, even when

things aren't going perfectly.

19. Moon And Stars!

Hey love, look who's back again,

Your little one is still lost in the magic of your gifts, a world that feels insane.

The excitement you created was beyond measure,

But what you gave me exceeded all expectations, a true treasure.

You filled my birthday with infinite reasons to laugh,

But my love, every day with you is the best day by far.

You shared with me the reasons you chose me,

My darling, I don't need reasons to choose you,

You are perfect, and forever you'll be a permanent part of me.

You wrote down all the nicknames you gave me on a nut's shell,

And baby, if I gathered every nut and seed in this world,

It would still fall short of the names you truly deserve,

Because I see you in every beautiful thing the universe has to offer.

My sweet girl, you crafted the most beautiful bouquet for me,

And you know what? I tried to make one too,

But couldn't find a single flower that could match your beauty.

You drew a picture of the world we dream of,

And I'm so obsessed with it, darling, it's now all around me,

So whenever I look at it, it'll be you that I see first.

Your packaged surprise left me in tears, my love,

You always said my efforts outweighed yours,

But now, I am forever your debtor,

Grateful for everything, and for all that you've given me.

You wrote the most precious letter in the world,

Saying I'm the best thing that's happened to you,

But love, you got it wrong; it's you who are the best thing that's ever happened to me.

You called me the prettiest soul, but again, my darling,

When I asked the butterflies, they flew close and whispered a name that wasn't mine,

And after they spoke, they shone brighter, more beautiful,

I think we both know whose name it was, don't we?

Unfortunately, honey, I have nothing to return as a gift,

I tried to catch fireflies for you, but when I compared them to your eyes,

They seemed so dim, so unworthy of the brilliance you hold.

I tried to collect rain for you, but when I tasted it next to your tears,

The rain tasted bitter in comparison to your sweetness.

I tried to bring the moon to you, but it was nowhere to be found,

And the stars whispered that it disappeared,

Because your beauty made even the moon feel insecure.

I tried to take a peacock's crown to claim you as my queen,

But your love stopped me from hurting another living being.

So, here's what I have for you, my love:

A simple kiss, soft and sincere,

Just place your lips on mine and feel the world melt away,

A kiss to celebrate everything we are, everything we share.

I give you myself, the most imperfect being, to make him whole,

I give you a weak man to make him strong,

I give you a child, only craving your love and care,

I give you a writer whose every story has always been about you.

I give you a man who was lost but now belongs only to you.

Baby, just one more gift, one more promise,
Never leave me, even when I'm alone with myself,
For without you, I am afraid of who I am.
Hold my hand, rub your palm against mine,
Come closer, let me feel your breath as you feel mine.
Make my life colorful, take away my scars,
Honey, I'm still under the spell of your drawing,
So let's lie under the open sky,
Your head on my shoulder, watching the moon and stars.

Trivia For 'Moon and Stars'

"Moon and Stars" is a poem I wrote for my girlfriend as a heartfelt thanksgiving for the incredible gifts she gave me on my birthday. It holds a special place in my heart because, after a long time, I felt like I had truly written one of my classic, signature poems- raw, simple, yet profoundly beautiful. It's filled with the signature elements that have come to define my writing: butterflies, fireflies, the moon, and the stars. These are the symbols that always appear when I'm trying to capture the magic and beauty she brings into my life.

The poem was inspired by the gifts she gave me, which were so precious and thoughtful that when I tried to find something worthy to give her in return, I felt completely inadequate. I went looking for a gift to match hers, but everything seemed to fall short. The love and effort she put into her presents made everything I tried to do feel small and insignificant. The gifts she gave me were not just material things, they were pieces of her heart. That's what made them so rare, so invaluable. In the poem, I tried to convey the overwhelming sense of being in her debt, not because of the physical gifts, but because of the emotional depth they represented.

The fireflies, the butterflies, the moon and the stars, these symbols are my way of reflecting how her presence in my life shines brighter than anything I could ever give her in return. The moon, which she made the stars feel insecure, the fireflies that can't compete with the brightness of her eyes, and the butterflies that whisper her name, all of these elements come from my heart as I try to express how deeply she touches me. It's a testament to how magical she makes me feel and how, despite everything I've done, I feel like

I am forever indebted to her. It's also a reminder that love isn't about equal exchanges. Sometimes, the beauty of a gift lies in its simplicity and in the feelings it evokes. And in my case, the love she gives me is worth more than anything I could ever return.

20. Beneath The Ocean!

In the depths where the oceans sing,

A love as vast as the sea's wide ring.

Coral reefs with colors bold,

Mirror a bond that will never grow cold.

Like kelp that sways with the ocean's song,

Our hearts entwined, where we belong.

The currents whisper secrets of grace,

A love that dances in this sacred space.

With every ripple, every wave,

Our hearts, like tides, are wild and brave.

The ocean's rhythm guides us true,

As stars above, our love renews.

A galaxy of fish, so bright,

Reflects the stars in the endless night.

Underneath the shimmering sea,

You and I are meant to be.

Beneath the surface, where dreams reside,

We sail together, side by side.

Through kelp forests and caverns deep,

Our love is the treasure we vow to keep.

The moon above, the tide below,

In this vast, eternal flow.

No boundary between sea and sky,

Just you and me, reaching high.

In the quiet depths, our souls converge,

A cosmic pulse, a love's great surge.
The ocean's heart beats strong and deep,
A love that's ours to cherish and keep.
The sea is vast, but never lonely,
With you, I am never the only.
From the sunlit waves to the darkest abyss,
Our love is endless, a boundless kiss.
Through ocean trenches and starlit skies,
We swim together where infinity lies.
Your eyes, like constellations, shine,
Guiding me through the depths divine.
Like bioluminescent creatures' glow,
Your love lights the path where I go.
From the surface to the abyss so wide,
With you, I have nothing to hide.
In the silence of the deep blue sea,
I find my peace, I find you and me.
Like stars that twinkle through the night,
Our love is a beacon, pure and bright.
The ocean's vastness, the sky's endless grace,
Are but a reflection of your face.
And as we dive into love's great tide,
We soar through space, side by side.
The currents carry us far and wide,
In this boundless love, we'll forever ride.
Like ships that sail beneath the moon,
Our hearts will sail through time's sweet tune.
With you, I am whole, my soul set free,
Our love, like the sea, eternally.

No end in sight, no beginning, no end,

In this ocean of love, you are my friend.

Through galaxies and ocean floor,

We will discover love ever more.

A treasure deep within the stars,

Your love, my compass, forever ours.

No earthly measure, no cosmic tide,

Could ever tear us apart, divide.

Together, we dive into the deep,

In the infinite love we promise to keep.

Trivia For 'Beneath The Ocean'

"Beneath the Ocean" is a poem I wrote imagining a world beneath the ocean, where I describe how the lover would love his girlfriend in an underwater realm. The poem is full of rich underwater imagery, from the deep blue currents to coral reefs, and the idea of the love existing among the sea creatures, hidden in the heart of the ocean. It's a testament to the fact that no matter what world they inhabit, whether it's Earth or some other faraway universe, his love for her would remain the same, deep, infinite, and obsessive.

One of the most beautiful things about this poem is the way I used the ocean as a metaphor for the love. The ocean, with its vastness and mystery, symbolizes how the love feels, endless, timeless, and full of hidden wonders. The creatures of the deep, the swaying kelp, and the peaceful currents represent the quiet, unwavering nature of our bond. In this imaginary underwater world, I picture us existing in harmony, as our love flows through the sea like an eternal current.

An interesting and unique fact about this poem is that it is the first one where I have used very few of my usual signature elements, like butterflies, fireflies, or the moon and stars. Instead, I focused on the aquatic theme, creating a new kind of imagery, yet the essence of the poem is still deeply connected to the emotions I want to express, love that transcends time, place, and even the boundaries of reality itself. Ultimately, "Beneath the Ocean" is not just an exploration of love in a fictional world; it's a powerful declaration that no matter where we are, I will always love her with the same depth and devotion, because our love is infinite, just like the ocean itself.

21. Us In Every Universe!

In the deep blue where the oceans sing,

Beneath the waves, our hearts take wing.

In currents that swirl like endless time,

I'd find you, love, in the brine.

We'd breathe in the silence of the sea,

In a world where the sky's a distant plea,

Where coral reefs cradle our hearts so near,

And whispers of love are all we'd hear.

On Mercury's scorched, trembling face,

I'd search for you in the heat and space.

Under skies where the stars burn bright,

We'd love through the fire of endless light.

Your hand, a shadow on the blinding sand,

Our hearts entwined, we'd still understand.

Though the air is thin, and the days are few,

Mercury's warmth could never outshine you.

On Venus, where the skies are thick with gold,

We'd walk through storms that never grow old.

In the crushing clouds, where the heat will soar,

We'd love each other like never before.

In the weight of the world, in the thick of the haze,

We'd find our path through the foggy maze.

Even the clouds can't obscure our light,

I'd hold you close through every endless night.

On Earth, where the flowers bloom and fade,

We'd live and love in every shade.

In the sunlight's glow or under moon's embrace,

Every moment with you, a tender grace.

Through fields of gold and mountains high,

I'd keep you close, under the same sky.

The world may change, seasons may turn,

But in your love, forever I'll burn.

On the Moon, where the silence is deep,

I'd hold you close in the stars' quiet sweep.

Our footprints etched in dust and stone,

We'd be the only ones, never alone.

Beneath the stars, we'd share a dance,

A love so pure, a cosmic trance.

In the endless void, we'd stand side by side,

For even the stars can't hide our pride.

On Mars, where the red sands stretch wide,

I'd love you through the storms that never subside.

With two hearts beating in a distant land,

We'd make our home in that barren sand.

Through dust and dreams, we'd carve our place,

Love's light shining in the Martian space.

Even the cold can't freeze our hearts,

For love on Mars still never departs.

On Uranus, where the winds howling freeze,

I'd love you through the cosmic breeze.

In the icy sky where the colors swirl,

We'd float together, a boy and girl.

Through rings of blue and skies so pale,

Our love would sail like a comet's tail.

No matter how cold the universe may be,
With you, my love, I'd always be free.
On Saturn, where the rings stretch far,
I'd gaze at you under distant stars.
In the shadow of moons, so graceful and pure,
We'd find a love that would always endure.
The beauty of rings, the light of the sky,
Could never compare to the gleam in your eye.
Through Saturn's moons, we'd spin and fly,
A love unbroken, till the stars die.
On Neptune, where the winds blow wild,
I'd be your anchor, you my child.
In the deep blue, where the ice meets the sky,
I'd hold you close, no need to ask why.
Through the storms and the depths of the sea,
Our love would echo for eternity.
Even the oceans can't swallow our grace,
We'd find our rhythm in Neptune's embrace.
And here, in the universe we now hold dear,
In the quiet, I find your heartbeat near.
No matter where the stars may fly,
Our love will always touch the sky.
In every universe, through time and space,
I'll love you forever, in every place.
For where we are, no distance or time,
Could ever break our endless rhyme.
In this life, or one beyond the stars,
We'll always be, no matter how far.
For you and I, in any space,

Are love's eternal, timeless grace.

Trivia For 'Us In Every Universe'

"Us in Every Universe" is a poem I wrote after finalizing the content of this book, but its true inspiration came from a very personal place. I needed to remind both myself and her of the depth and beauty of our connection, no matter the storms we face. The idea for the poem came as I thought about how, no matter where we are, whether on Mercury, Venus, Earth, or beyond, our love would always remain perfect. It was a way for me to express that despite our differences and disagreements, we are truly meant to be together, no matter the universe we inhabit.

The poem weaves through different planets and universes, beginning with Mercury, and touches on each celestial body, from Venus to Neptune, to show that in every corner of the cosmos, our love will persist, unwavering and unbreakable. It's an exploration of how our connection transcends time and space, and how, even in different worlds, we remain the same passionate couple. This is a powerful testament to the theme of cosmic and celestial love that runs throughout the rest of my book, and it fits perfectly within the larger narrative of thelove story.

It's my way of telling the world that if the love is true and pure then no matter what happens, you are perfect together in every universe. I chose to add this poem to the storyline because it aligns with the themes of the book, love that is eternal and celestial, always surviving, always thriving, even in the most unlikely of places.In essence, "Us in Every Universe" serves as a reminder that our love isn't bound by anything, not even the vastness of space. No matter what battles we face or where we are in life, our connection remains pure, perfect, and infinite. It's a poem that speaks to the heart of every relationship, one that, like the stars and planets, will continue to shine brightly, no matter where we are.

22. Missing You On That Old Bench!

Do you remember, love, how we first met,
In junior class, where destiny was set?
Two young souls, innocent and true,
A boy and a girl, and a friendship that grew.
That bench we shared, a sacred place,
Where time stood still, in its gentle embrace.
Whispers of laughter, secrets exchanged,
Innocence and wonder, never estranged.
We'd pass our tiffins, sharing bites,
Trading stories under the schoolyard lights.
Dreams of tomorrow, we'd endlessly weave,
Under the gaze of the moon, we'd believe.
You, with your eyes so bright, so bold,
Dominating, fierce, a sight to behold.
I'd smile as you took charge, my heart a flutter,
Your voice a melody, like a wind's soft mutter.
We spoke of a future, where we'd fly,
Stargazing beneath the velvet sky.
Fireflies danced, like tiny lanterns in flight,
Guiding our dreams through the endless night.
Butterflies would flit, in the warmth of the day,
As if they too knew, our hearts' secret way.
And in those moments, pure and sweet,
We shared our poetry, incomplete yet complete.

The school uniform, with its stripes so neat,
Would become a memory, so tender, so fleet.
But sitting there, side by side, so fine,
You'd rest your head, and I'd rest mine.
And now, I miss that simple, precious time,
When our laughter was endless, and our love sublime.
The bench, the whispers, the stories we spun,
How I long to relive them, those days in the sun.
Now here I sit, in the quiet of night,
Missing your presence, your spark, your light.
The moon watches over, as I close my eyes,
And I feel you there, where memory lies.
Rest your lips on mine, and let me go back,
To the days of innocence, to the childhood track.
To the bench that held our hearts and dreams,
To the love that started, so tender, so pure, it seems.
With every breath, I remember the way,
We loved so simply, day after day.
A love that grew, and a bond so true,
From the first day in class, to me and you.
The schoolyard's whispers, the laughter that roamed,
Are echoes of a time that feels like home.
And though we've grown, and the years have flown,
My heart is still yours, in the place we've known.
And as Tom and Jerry, in their playful chase,
Bounded through trials, yet never lost their place,
So, my love, though we've wandered, and time may stray,
My heart will forever find you, come what may.

Trivia For 'Missing You On That Old Bench'

"Missing You on That Old Bench" is a poem that holds a very special place in my heart, as it reflects a memory that is both nostalgic and deeply emotional. It captures the essence of how a simple friendship, full of innocence, transformed into something far deeper, a childhood romance that blossomed into a lifelong partnership. The "old bench" in the poem symbolizes the place where it all began, the setting where we would spend countless hours together, talking, laughing, and dreaming about our futures.

In this poem, the lover tells his girlfriend, "I miss us on that old bench." It was a recurring thought, a moment of reflection on how far they've come and how much has changed, yet how certain things, like their bond, have remained constant. The old bench is more than just a physical space, it represents the purity and simplicity of their early days together, when they were best friends who didn't yet realize that one day, they'd be partners for life. Also there is reference of 'Tom and Jerry' which describes the childhood days.

I wrote this poem as a way to revisit those cherished memories, to relive the innocence of childhood, and to express how that innocent love gradually transformed into the passionate, unwavering connection we share today.

"Missing You on That Old Bench" takes readers on an emotional rollercoaster, filled with both the sweetness of nostalgia and the depth of a love that has evolved over time. It reminds us that true love isn't something that happens overnight, it's a journey, a gradual transition from friendship to romance, and then to lifelong partnership.

This poem also fits into the larger theme of the book because it showcases how passionate love doesn't simply emerge in a moment, but rather, it's built over years, rooted in shared experiences and the small moments that shape who we are as individuals and as a couple. The story of our childhood, and how it set the foundation for the love we share now, is a testament to the idea that the most meaningful relationships are often those that have had time to grow and mature. In short, "Missing You on That Old Bench" is more than just a reflection on the past; it's a celebration of the love that has withstood the test of time, starting from the most innocent beginnings and blossoming into a passionate, enduring connection that will last forever.

23. Firefly's Whisper!

Beneath the velvet cloak of night,

Where fireflies waltz in silver light,

We stroll, our hearts in quiet rhyme,

As time stands still, embracing time.

The moon, a painter, paints the skies,

As stars, like whispers, softly rise,

Each step we take in love's sweet trance,

The night responds, a gentle dance.

Hand in hand, we chase the glow,

Of fireflies that come and go,

Their tiny lights like distant dreams,

As if they're caught in moonlit beams.

We laugh, you and I, so carefree,

Your voice, a melody to me,

We run, we race, in sweet pursuit,

Of glowing wings that seem like Suicune..

I reach for you, but you're ahead,

You turn to smile, then quickly tread,

Your laughter sparkles in the air,

A song the night has come to share.

The fireflies blink, they softly gleam,

And we, two souls, are part of their dream,

You pause and catch one in your hand,

A fleeting glow, like love so grand.

I look at you, and in your eyes,

I see the endless starry skies,
A universe where we belong,
Where we are free, where we are strong.
In the distance, a light appears,
A single flash that calms our fears,
It flickers once, then fades away,
Like a message from another day.
I smile, recalling a tale once told,
Of a signal light, bright and bold,
Like Gordon's signal in the dark,
Calling Batman with a single spark.
But here, beneath this sky so wide,
It's not a hero we need to find,
It's you, my love, my shining star,
No signal needed, you are my heart.
As we walk, the night is ours,
The fireflies twirl in endless showers,
But something strange stirs in the air,
A subtle feeling, a whisper shared.
A firefly lands upon your cheek,
It flickers, twirls, and starts to speak,
Its tiny voice so soft and bright,
A secret whispered through the night.
"I envy you," it seems to say,
As we continue on our way,
"For in her smile, I see the sun,
While I, a glow, am but undone."
"It's true," the firefly softly sighs,
"Her smile outshines the endless skies.

Her glow is brighter than our light,
And in her presence, we take flight."
I stop, I listen, and I smile,
As if the firefly knew all the while,
That in your smile, I found my bliss,
A love too perfect, sealed with a kiss.
So we continue, the night so sweet,
Our hearts entwined, our spirits meet,
The fireflies whisper in the air,
That nothing compares to what we share.
And as we walk, side by side,
The stars and moon become our guide,
And somewhere, in the soft night's kiss,
A firefly's envy fades in bliss.
For in your smile, my world is bright,
More than any firefly's light.

Trivia For 'Firefly's Whisper'

"Firefly's Whisper" is a poem that holds a unique and deeply personal significance to me. In this poem, I've used fireflies not just as simple creatures of nature, but as symbols of light, glow, and romance. The idea of fireflies whispering in jealousy because they can't match the brightness of the girlfriend's glow is a poetic way to express how her presence outshines everything around her. It's a playful yet poignant metaphor that underscores the special and luminous qualities she has in lover's life. The fireflies, who have always been a central element in my poetry, now find themselves envious of the brilliance she exudes, which brings a layer of depth to both the poem and the overall theme of my work.

This poem is, in many ways, a thanksgiving to fireflies. I've always had a deep connection to them, they represent so much more than just insects to me. They're a symbol of love, light, and quiet beauty. For me, fireflies are not just decorative elements; they are companions in my world of poetry. They've played a significant role in many of my poems, including in this book, where they add a certain glow to the atmosphere, much like the girlfriend brings brightness into lover's life. They serve as my little partners in this creative journey, and I feel they bring a certain magic that enhances the themes I explore, particularly the ideas of light, beauty, and the ethereal nature of love.

In this poem, I also wanted to celebrate how fireflies have elevated the theme of my entire book. Their quiet glow has become a metaphor for love itself: constant, beautiful, and, in many ways, unassuming yet powerful. The presence of fireflies in all my poems acts as a thread connecting the different emotional landscapes I've explored. Whether as the backdrop of a peaceful night, as symbols of love's light, or as creatures that bring magic to the mundane, fireflies continue to add a sense of wonder and depth to my writing. Ultimately, "Firefly's Whisper" is a tribute to both the creatures and the light they represent in my life, both in the literal sense and as an essential part of my creative process. It is a celebration of the brightness they bring, and a reflection on how, in my poetic world, fireflies will always be my companions, guiding me through the glow of love and creativity.

24. Butterfly Couple!

From a humble cocoon, so small and concealed,

A life unfolds, delicately revealed.

A tiny being, wings tender and new,

Bathed in the morning's golden hue.

With a flutter, a breath, a shiver of flight,

He emerges into a world so bright.

A butterfly, radiant, born to soar,

A story of love, of life, and more.

He flutters through the meadows, a vision so pure,

Drawn by a scent, so sweet, so sure.

There, in a dance of colors and light,

He spots her, a beauty in flight.

Her wings, adorned with hues of dawn,

A painting of life, so gracefully drawn.

They meet mid-air, a kiss on the breeze,

Two hearts beating in synchronized ease.

They dance in the sky, in a delicate waltz,

Each movement perfect, no need for a halt.

Through fields of wildflowers, under skies so wide,

They twirl and glide, side by side.

In the golden glow of the day's embrace,

They share silent words in the warmth of space.

Together they explore, from flower to tree,

The world's wonders, wild and free.

When the sun dips low, and the stars awake,

They nestle close, in a soft, warm stake.
In the whisper of the night, with moon's silver light,
They whisper dreams, both tender and bright.
He speaks of places they've yet to see,
Of mountains, rivers, and the vast sea.
She replies with a flutter, a gentle sigh,
Their love, a promise that will never die.
The days pass like petals falling slow,
And with each season, their love does grow.
They build a nest, a safe little place,
Where they dream of tomorrow, in the softest embrace.
New life stirs, in the still of dawn,
A tiny being, fragile and drawn.
A butterfly, small, with wings yet to find,
A part of their love, so tender and kind.
And as the little one learns to fly,
The parents watch, with joy in their eye.
Their wings spread wide, ready to soar,
A journey begins, forever more.
They teach their child to dance on air,
To find the beauty, to always care.
To flutter close, through wind and rain,
To cherish love, through joy and pain.
Oh, how a real couple can learn from their song,
To love so deeply, to be strong.
To find beauty in the simplest of things,
To dance together, let their hearts take wings.
To hold each other, when night is long,
To sing their own love, an endless song.

Like the butterflies, who fly and create,

A love that endures, that won't abate.

So, let us learn from their light-hearted grace,

From their love that time cannot erase.

Let us love with joy, with wings so wide,

And in life's dance, stand side by side.

In the simplest moments, in the wind's gentle hum,

Find the beauty, the love, and let it come.

For in each flutter, in each shared gaze,

We find a love that will never faze.

Trivia For 'Butterfly Couple'

"Butter Couple" is a deeply symbolic and beautiful poem that takes the readers on a journey through the life cycle of butterflies, using their transformation as a metaphor for the growth and evolution of love between two people. In this poem, I personify butterflies to depict the stages of a lover's journey, from birth, to growth, to finding a mate, and ultimately, to creating something new. The butterflies' life cycle mirrors the path of a relationship: starting from the innocent beginnings of love, transforming and evolving through challenges, and finally finding harmony and the ability to create something lasting and beautiful together.

This poem is not just a love story; it is a celebration of the delicate, beautiful, and transformative nature of love itself. Just as butterflies undergo an incredible metamorphosis, so too do the hearts of lovers, shifting and growing through time, becoming something more than they were at the start. The way butterflies find each other and form pairs, creating life together, perfectly mirrors how lovers come together, build a life, and create memories and legacies that continue beyond themselves.

The poem is also a thanksgiving to butterflies, creatures that have long been symbolic in my work and in my heart. Butterflies have been vital to both the storyline of this book and my poetry as a whole. They are symbols of change, beauty, fragility, and the grace of transformation. Over the years, they have played an essential role in my writing, enhancing the themes of love, growth, and the passage of time. I have used butterflies to represent the beauty of connection, the delicacy of emotions, and the quiet, powerful way that love evolves and takes root.

Ultimately, "Butter Couple" is not just a poem about butterflies, it is a poem about the journey of love itself. It is about how two souls, like butterflies, begin their journey as fragile, innocent creatures, then transform and find each other, creating a bond that is powerful enough to withstand time. This poem, like many of the others in the book, celebrates the beauty and fragility of love, and the way it grows and evolves, just as butterflies do through their life cycle. It is a tribute to both the butterflies that have been such an important part of my creative journey and to the love that, like the butterfly, has the power to transform and flourish in the most beautiful ways.

25. The Burnt Pages Of Your Diary!

Words were so light and half erased,

Resembling a story so beautiful but imperfect,

Ink was disappearing from the paper,

Paper was cooked like it never existed.

The book in my hand was burnt to the extent,

That Charizard's existence seemed real.

Ashes of the paper were hard to gather,

But it seemed the emotions while writing were so real to raise the phoenix.

Those stories on the burnt paper were something peaceful and real,

Maybe it was the best blend of poetry and reality, but it was not clear.

It's sad I don't have the fresh pages to unfold the greatest love story,

All I can do is to read the book as Keller saw the world.

Burnt completely, yet an aroma so familiar and close to my heart,

Holding that half-cooked diary seemed like holding a ripped heart.

The first page had some nostalgic touch,

I remember the warmth of those classroom moments,

The quiet hum of the school bell,

When we would sneak glances, eyes catching,

And our hearts would race without sound,

Your laughter would echo like sunlight filtering through autumn leaves,

Those fleeting touches, secret whispers,

A childhood romance born under the shade of schoolyard trees.

The ink, so fragile, must have painted those memories,
Of shared sandwiches, of pencils passed like promises,
Of fleeting moments before life was complicated.
Then, the pages spoke of the future,
A vision of endless skies and quiet nights,
Of stargazing together, wrapped in the warmth of each other's presence,
Lying on the grass, faces tilted toward the cosmos,
Chasing constellations as if we could catch them.
We'd walk along moonlit paths, my hand in yours,
Our silhouettes dancing under the pale glow of a thousand dreams.
You imagined me writing poetry for you,
Each line an ode to your beauty, to your heart.
We'd write books together, exploring mountains, oceans,
Each chapter more adventurous than the last,
Fulfilling the promises made on paper,
Completing our bucket list, each line more vibrant than the last.
But then, the edges were burnt,
And all I could see was the faint outline of our first kiss,
The soft touch of lips as the world disappeared around us.
Our first date, the quiet tension before the magic,
You in that dress, like a star falling to earth,
And the rose I gave you, the petals of which still haunt me.
Our first hug, so simple, yet it held the weight of everything.
Every first moment written in those pages,
The first time you smiled at me like I was the only one in the world,
The first time I knew I loved you,
The first time you said it back.
And then, the pages where we were not yet together,

Where I sent you nature photographs,

The mountain views, the sunsets,

All those moments wrapped in images,

So you could feel the beauty I wanted to share with you,

Poems written under the stars,

I sent them to you with the hope that my words could reach you,

Even when miles apart.

You'd wait for weekends, eagerly calling me from your hostel,

Telling me all the stories, the gossips that made me laugh,

I could hear the joy in your voice,

Like the sound of the rain after a drought.

And there was that day,

On my birthday, I finally told you "I love you",

My heart in my hands,

But you were too nervous to say it back.

I understood then, but it still hurt.

As I held the burnt pages, I could see you flexing my poems,

Showing your friends how I spoke of dreams,

Of the book I would one day write for you,

Of the promises in my verses,

How you believed in every word,

Telling them, "One day, he will fulfill it all."

We'd grow old together,

My poems and your laughter would echo through the years.

A life filled with love and promises kept,

Where nothing could stand between us.

But then, the pages began to blur with the heat of betrayal,

The ink smudged as the flames grew stronger.

You wrote about what I did to you,

How I shattered your heart with the weight of my mistakes.
You felt cheated, like the trust we had built was a fragile thread
That snapped under the strain of my immaturity.
The guilt gnaws at me as I read these words,
Words that cut deeper than the flames that consumed them.
You wrote of the nights you spent crying,
Of how I destroyed what we had,
How my actions ripped apart a dream that was only beginning.
You were devastated, lost,
And I couldn't see the wreckage I had caused until it was too late.
You lived without me for months,
Rebuilding, healing, but the scars remained.
And in that moment, I realized what the diary truly was,
A testament to all that we could have been,
A chronicle of a love that was real,
Yet poisoned by the very hands that promised to protect it.
And so, you burned it.
You burned it, because what else was there to do?
The paper was no longer a record of love,
But a reminder of promises broken,
A shrine to the ruins of us.
In the ashes, I find my regret,
Not in the fire, but in the moments that led to it.
I wish I could rewrite the story,
But all that remains is this half-burnt memory.

Trivia For 'The Burnt Pages Of Your Diary'

This poem holds a very special place in my heart because it marks the moment I first became truly emotional while writing. It reflects a real-life event that was both heart-wrenching and transformative, one that profoundly shaped my relationship and my journey as a writer. The inspiration behind the poem comes from a diary my girlfriend kept when we were just friends. Unfortunately, the diary was burned. The burning of the diary was both a way of releasing the pain and, in a way, a final goodbye to the love that was, at that point, shattered.

Since I never got the chance to read the diary before it was destroyed, this poem became my way of imagining what she might have written. It blends poetry with imagination, capturing the essence of the love story that was lost, the memories we shared, and the dreams of a future that would never come to be in that form. In a way, it serves as a tribute to the unspoken, a reflection on all the things I never had the chance to read or experience. One of the most significant aspects of this poem is that it marks a departure from my usual writing style. For the first time, I present the lover not as the romantic hero but as the villain, acknowledging the mistakes I made and the heartbreak I caused. This shift in perspective was both difficult and cathartic, as it forced me to face the consequences of my actions and the pain I inflicted.

The poem is also rich with symbolic references, each of which adds depth to the narrative. The 'Charizard reference represents both strength and destruction, symbolizing how something once beautiful, like the diary, was consumed by the flames of my actions. The Phoenix, a creature of rebirth and healing, mirrors the emotional journey of recovery after betrayal. The mention of Helen Keller is a metaphor for how I had to "read" the remnants of the burnt diary, understanding its emotional weight without fully seeing its contents. The recurring image of the 'burnt pages' not only represents the physical remnants of the diary but also the emotional residue of regret and lost opportunities. These symbols reflect the complexity of the situation, the destruction, the hope for renewal, and the lingering impact of my mistakes.

As the poem unfolds, it traces the arc of our relationship: from innocent schoolyard moments to the early stages of love, followed by the heartache of betrayal, and ultimately to the acceptance of the aftermath. It explores not just the joy of love but also the painful reality of mistakes and the difficult process of healing. The narrative reflects a love story that is both beautiful and flawed, capturing the imperfection of our shared journey. At its core, the poem is about regret, not only for the loss of the diary but also for the loss of trust, the emotional damage, and the time we lost due to my actions. The ashes represent both the remnants of the diary and the lingering regret I feel in my heart.

In a way, this poem is a gift to my girlfriend, a way of sharing with her a piece of my soul, my journey of growth, and my deep remorse. It is my way of acknowledging the pain I caused and expressing my hope for the future we now share. Writing this poem was my way of saying, "I understand the pain I caused, but I'm here now, and I'm not going anywhere." Ultimately, this poem is more than just words, it is a testament to love, loss, and

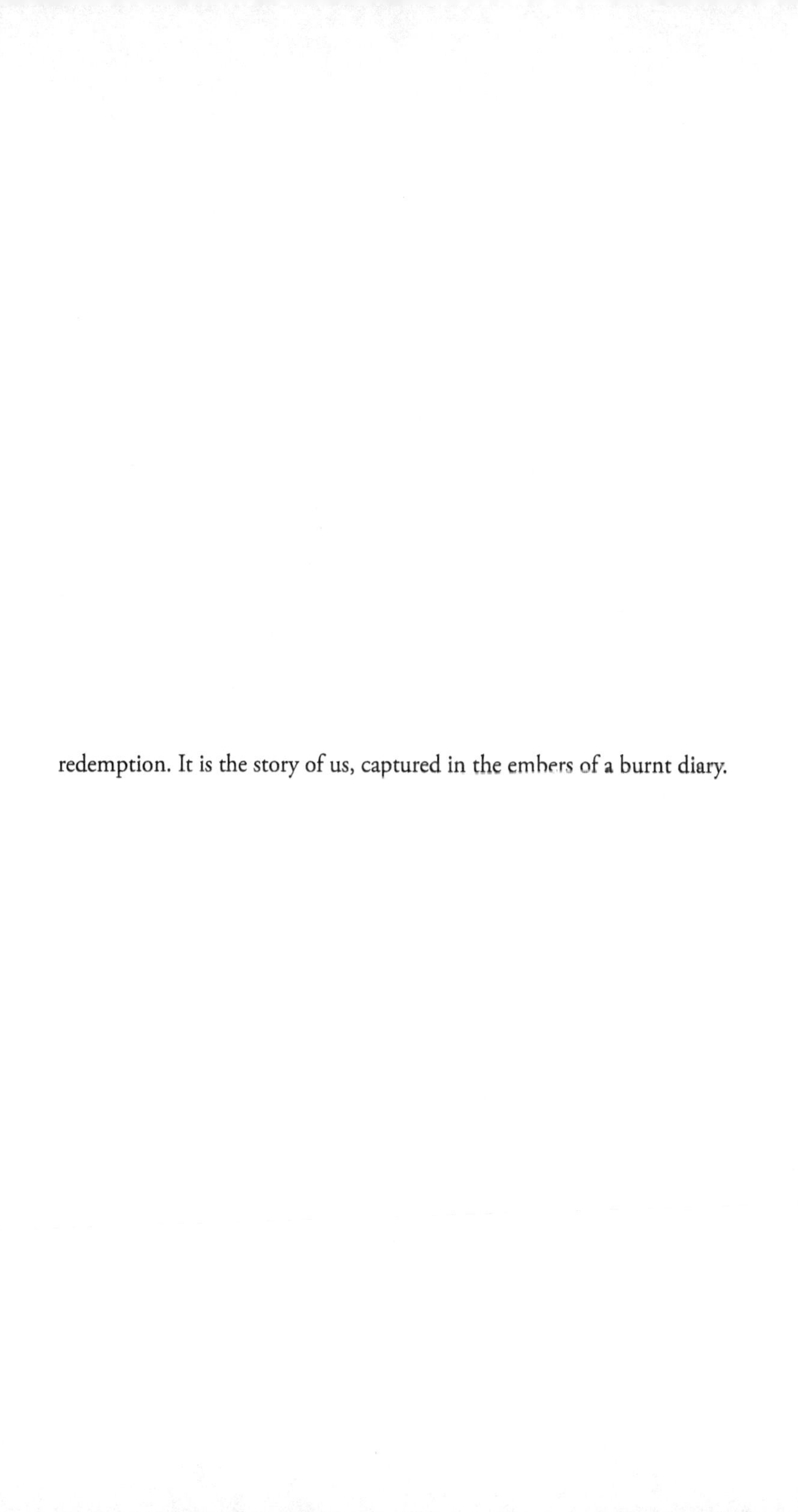

redemption. It is the story of us, captured in the embers of a burnt diary.

26. Hakuna Matata!

In the sun-drenched plains, where the golden grasses sway,

Life unfolds in a dance, with no need for dismay.

With you by my side, each dawn's a new song,

A journey through the wild where we both belong.

When we walk through the savanna, each step feels right,

With the warmth of our laughter, brighter than the light.

As Timon and Pumbaa once sang, so carefree and free,

"Life's not a worry, it's a paradise for you and me."

When shadows fall, and the night seems too long,

When the world's chorus is an unfamiliar song,

I have you to lean on, my shelter, my friend,

Together we face the trials, until the very end.

You lift me up, like Mufasa's gentle call,

When I'm lost and frightened, you're there to break my fall.

We stand shoulder to shoulder, like kings in the wild,

With hearts so pure, untamed, and mild.

Like the guardian angel who watches from above,

You guide me with wisdom, with patience, and love.

You're the light in my path when darkness arrives,

A constant reminder of how hope survives.

With strength that echoes, as mighty as the sky,

You remind me, like Mufasa, that I am never alone, and never shy.

Your voice, a chorus that keeps me strong,

Your presence, a melody I've known all along.

But not all is perfect in our world of bliss,

"

There are shadows that lurk, with threats we can't miss.
Like Scar's deceit, there are whispers of doubt,
Negative voices that seek to turn love inside out.
They try to break what we've built, to ruin the scene,
To pull us apart and make our spirits lean.
But together we stand, defying the night,
Our bond is our shield, our collective fight.
If troubles arise, like hyenas in the night,
We stand as one, ready for the fight.
You remind me of my path, with wisdom so true,
Guarding my steps, like Rafiki, guiding me through.
When I stray from the light, you hold my hand,
Teaching me that love is the strongest stand.
In a world that spins fast, where chaos can spread,
With you, my love, I fear nothing ahead.
The worries of life fade when we share each day,
Like Simba and Nala, with joy in our play.
No storm can shake us, no darkness can reign,
Because our bond is a flame that will never wane.
With you, there's no need for shadows or doubt,
Every moment's a treasure, a reason to shout.
Every laugh, every tear, every step that we take,
With you, my partner, there's no mistake.
We hold onto goodness, our souls intertwined,
Our love is a promise that's forever enshrined.
Together we face what life has to give,
With you, I know I'll always live.
As we sing, as we dance, as we fight and we heal,
Hakuna Matata is not just a dream, it's real.

So when the world whispers that we should be afraid,
We'll smile, knowing we've got it made.
For in your eyes, I see the truth, pure and clear,
With you, there's no worry, no need for fear.
Hakuna Matata.

Trivia For 'Hakuna Matata'

"Hakuna Matata" is a poem inspired by a core belief that resonates deeply within me: the importance of having a motto in a relationship that keeps you grounded, resilient, and free from unnecessary worries. The title, of course, draws from the famous song in "The Lion King", which became a symbol of carefree living and embracing life's challenges with a positive, carefree attitude. In this poem, I take that very philosophy and weave it into the fabric of a relationship, one where no matter the struggles or obstacles, the motto "Hakuna Matata", meaning "no worries", becomes a guiding principle.

The poem is filled with references to "The Lion King", one of my favorite films and a timeless source of inspiration. It's a story about resilience, love, and the strength of connection, messages that are beautifully reflected in this poem. The imagery of the savanna, the warmth of shared laughter, and the idea of walking together through life's trials all echo the spirit of the film, where characters like Timon, Pumbaa, Mufasa, Rafiki, and Simba remind us that love, loyalty, and strength can overcome any adversity.

Throughout the poem, I use these characters and their qualities to reflect the dynamic between two people facing life together. The carefree attitude of Timon and Pumbaa symbolizes the joy and simplicity in finding peace with each other. Mufasa's wisdom represents the strength and guidance one partner offers when the other feels lost. The image of Simba and Nala portrays the playful, unshakable bond shared between two people, no matter how fast the world spins around them. Even Scar's deceit is acknowledged as a metaphor for the challenges and negative forces that try to undermine love and happiness, but the message remains clear: together, we stand strong, and with "Hakuna Matata," we face everything together.

The poem isn't just a retelling of "The Lion King", it's a personal reflection of how love can be the most powerful force in helping you navigate life's ups and downs. It serves as a reminder that life will throw its challenges, like the hyenas or the shadows of doubt, but love and unity will always be the ultimate shield. The line "Hakuna Matata is not just a dream, it's real," is my way of saying that this carefree, worry-free life is achievable when you have the right person by your side.

In the end, "Hakuna Matata" is more than just a catchy phrase from a beloved film. It's a philosophy I carry into my own life and relationship. This poem is a tribute to that idea that no matter what life brings, we face it together with strength, love, and a commitment to never letting fear or doubt take hold. With the motto of 'Hakuna Matata' in our hearts, there's truly no need for worries, just joy, trust, and the assurance that we're in this together, always.

27. Paths We Have Yet To Wander!

There are paths we've yet to wander, untread and bright,
Hidden corners of the world, bathed in dream's light.
Places where snowflakes whisper secrets on the breeze,
And gondolas glide through the canals with ease.
Moments yet to come, so tender and sweet,
A future that waits, where our hearts will meet.
Two souls, bound by love's unspoken vow,
Looking ahead, to the "where" and the "how."
First, we'll journey to a land, vast and pure,
Antarctica, where silence is the heart's cure.
White expanses stretch as far as the eye can see,
A realm of ice, where we'll be wild and free.
I'll watch you dance with joy, your laughter bright,
As snowflakes fall in the pale twilight.
We'll wander hand in hand, across the frosted shore,
Where the world's whispers echo, peaceful and more.
We'll watch the penguins parade, their black-and-white suits,
As we share cocoa and stories, in our winter boots.
The aurora borealis will set the sky ablaze,
And in its shimmering dance, we'll stand amazed.
Under the ice-blue sky, I'll hold you close,
And tell you stories only the snow knows.
In the stillness of that frozen embrace,
I'll see the joy written on your face.

And then, we'll make our way to Venice, so grand,
A city of water, a dream made by hand.
With canals that glimmer under moonlight's glow,
And bridges that sing of love's soft flow.
We'll stroll through the Piazza San Marco's delight,
Where the pigeons flutter, and hearts take flight.
Hand in hand, we'll drift down canals so wide,
As gondoliers sing, with you as my guide.
We'll spend our afternoons in hidden cafes,
Sipping espresso, as the sunlight sways.
I'll write you poems on the backs of old maps,
Whispers of love, with romantic claps.
Venetian masks, a mystery to wear,
And in the masquerade, I'll see your eyes, so rare.
We'll share a kiss by the Bridge of Sighs,
As lovers' wishes soar to the skies.
And when the stars come out, painting the night,
We'll watch the moon, in its silver flight.
With the soft sound of water beneath our feet,
Venice and you, a love so sweet.
These journeys, my love, are more than just sights,
They're promises kept in the warmth of the nights.
They are paths we'll wander, and tales we'll weave,
Of moments cherished, of love we'll believe.
So let's dream, let's plan, let's set our course,
With hearts full of love, and a life we endorse.
Antarctica's peace, and Venice's song,
The paths we have yet to wander, where we both belong.
There, in the snow and the sun's gentle blaze,

We'll carve out our story, in life's tender maze.
And in each place, where our hearts will roam,
We'll find pieces of us, and call them home.

• 147 •

Trivia For 'Paths We Have Yet To Wander'

"Paths We Have Yet to Wander" is a deeply personal poem that reflects the dreams and aspirations of two people, the lover and his girlfriend, who are united not just by love, but by a shared vision of the future. This poem speaks to the dream of traveling to two places that hold special significance to them: 'Antarctica' and 'Venice'. In this storyline, these places are more than just travel destinations; they symbolize the journey of love, adventure, and the unique ways they connect with each other.

For lover, Venice represents romance, mystery, and timeless beauty. I've always been enchanted by its canals, its rich history, and the idea of being swept away by its quiet charm. For the girlfriend, Antarctica is a dream destination, a place of serenity and purity, where the silence of the snow and the vastness of the icy landscape offer a sense of peace and introspection. These places, so different from one another, mirror the balance they've found in their relationship, where contrasts exist, but they complement each other perfectly. The poem imagines their journey together through these contrasting landscapes, each experience shaped by the love they share.

In the first stanza, the poem speaks of the "paths we've yet to wander," an idea that reflects not just literal travel, but the life adventures they have yet to experience together. The imagery of snowflakes whispering secrets on the breeze and gondolas gliding through canals speaks to the intimacy and beauty they will encounter on these journeys. The "future that waits" is a promise of new memories, a life they will build side by side, moving forward with love and hope.

The references to Antarctica in the poem are woven with imagery of silence, ice, and freedom. I imagine myself walking hand-in-hand through the snow, experiencing the beauty of the landscape together, surrounded by the stillness of this frozen wonderland. The mention of penguins and the aurora borealis are direct allusions to the unique wildlife and natural wonders found in Antarctica, symbols of joy and wonder that will make our adventure unforgettable.

When the poem shifts to Venice, it becomes a celebration of romance, the mystery of Venetian masks, and the beauty of the city's canals. This part of the poem reflects my dream of wandering the labyrinth of Venice with my girlfriend, sharing quiet moments in hidden cafes and on gondola rides under the moonlit sky. The reference to The 'Merchant of Venice' through the Venetian masquerade adds a literary layer, with the idea of wearing masks evoking the mystery and complexity of love, and the emotional connections that go beyond appearances. In the poem, Venice isn't just a city we want to visit; it becomes a metaphor for the deeper layers of our relationship where secrets are shared, memories are made, and love is allowed to flourish freely.

The poem also touches on the idea of promise and commitment. These trips are more than just destinations; they represent the promises we make to one another, promises to explore the world together. Ultimately, "Paths We Have Yet to Wander" is a celebration of dreams, both personal and shared. For me, it's a love letter to my girlfriend, a reflection of the paths I hope we will walk together, the places we will see, and the love that will guide us

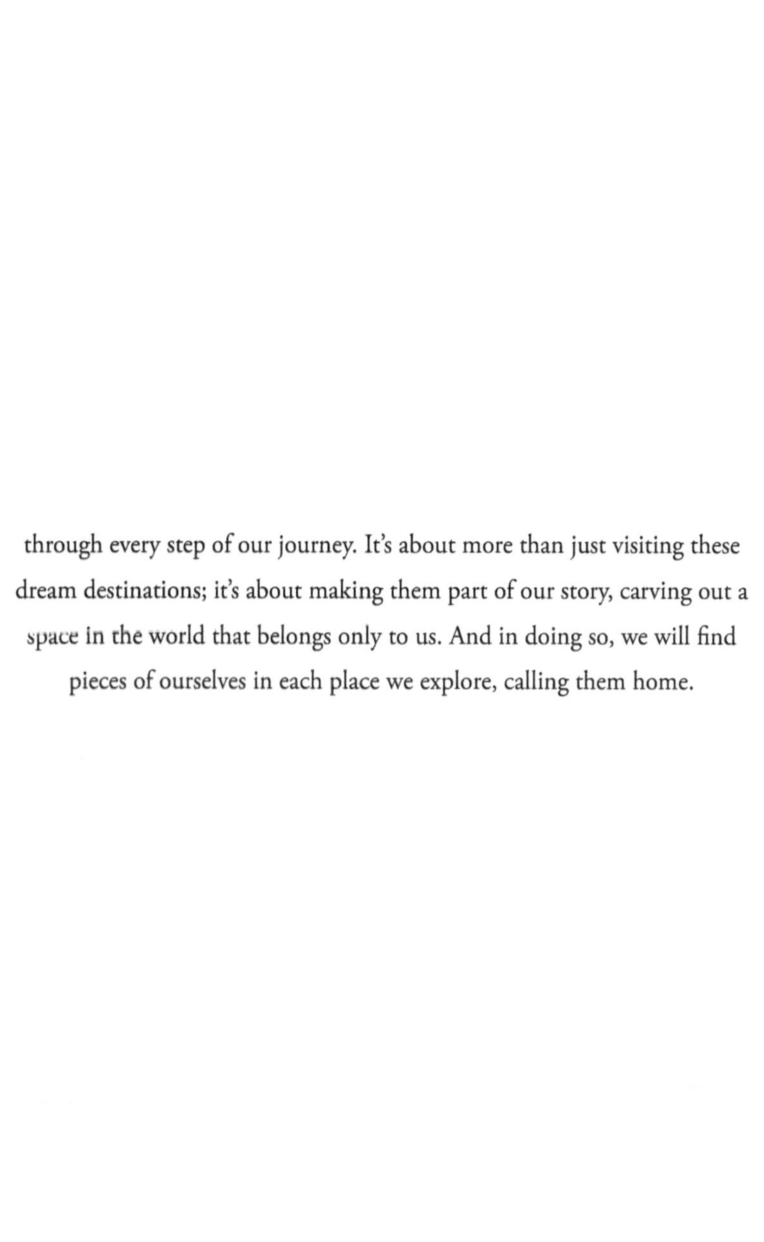

through every step of our journey. It's about more than just visiting these dream destinations; it's about making them part of our story, carving out a space in the world that belongs only to us. And in doing so, we will find pieces of ourselves in each place we explore, calling them home.

28. Our Bucket List Bliss!

Let's start with the stars, where we'll lay side by side,
Under the vast sky, our dreams as our guide.
Stargazing moments, with the moon's gentle glow,
A universe of promises, waiting to show.
We'll take night walks where silence meets sound,
Hand in hand, where love's truly found.
The first hug, the first kiss, electric and warm,
Our hearts beating fast, in the calm before the storm.
Our first rainfall, as droplets dance and play,
Laughing in the downpour, without a care or sway.
A first date, where we dress up and smile,
Each word, each glance, a memory to compile.
Holding hands for the very first time,
A touch so simple, yet perfectly sublime.
Playing in snow, a scene so pure and bright,
Snowflakes in your hair, hearts in flight.
Watching the sunset, as the day takes its bow,
Holding each other close, in the here and the now.
A trip to Antarctica, where the ice meets the sky,
Gliding through frozen beauty, you and I.
Venice awaits, with its canals and song,
We'll weave through the water, where we belong.
Exploring Delhi, with its chaos and charm,
A mix of the old, a pulse, a warm alarm.
First shopping spree, laughter in the aisles,

Picking out clothes, exchanging playful smiles.
A bike ride, wind in our hair, heart racing fast,
A moment of freedom, memories to last.
Kissing underwater, where time stands still,
A moment of magic, a rush, a thrill.
Cooking together, tasting our shared creation,
Skincare nights, soft laughter, relaxation.
Exchanging clothes, stealing a look,
A dress, a shirt, a playful hook.
Ziplining through forests, high and wild,
Screams of delight, the heart of a child.
Adopting a cat, a furry friend to hold,
A life together, stories untold.
Bonfire at the beach, stars reflected in the sea,
Walking on sand, just you and me.
A stay in the mountains, cozy and grand,
Cuddled up, with nature's hand.
Rooftop dates, the city beneath,
Slow dancing to music, our hearts in wreath.
Matching clothes, our favorite theme,
A glimpse of us, like a shared dream.
Swimming together, splashing in light,
Our laughter ringing, an endless delight.
Making reels, capturing our story,
A slow motion moment, a slice of glory.
Long car rides, with songs that we sing,
Chasing horizons, where the wild winds bring.
Attending each other's convocation, proud and loud,
Celebrating each victory, standing tall, unbowed.

Presenting a poem, your voice echoing clear,
A voiceover for love, a sound I'll always hear.
Cuddling close, watching you sleep,
Over video calls, when dreams run deep.
Pillow fights, laughter that won't end,
Tossing, turning, as we pretend.
Listening to songs through wired earphones,
Close together, where love's grown.
Late night ice cream, shared in delight,
Under the blanket of the moonlight.
Braiding your hair, a tender touch,
A simple act, meaning so much.
Our first proposal, with tears and smiles,
An eternal promise, crossing all miles.
Our first train ride, the rhythm of the track,
A journey together, no turning back.
Making hand impressions, a lasting mark,
A future we'll carve, in the light and dark.
These moments, this list, our dreams so grand,
Each one a memory, written by hand.
A lifetime of bliss, in your eyes I see,
The love story that's meant to be.
With every heartbeat, every dream, every wish,
We'll find our bliss, in our bucket list.

Trivia for 'Our Bucket List Bliss'

"Our Bucket List Bliss" is a deeply personal poem that captures the dreams, desires, and plans of a couple who are mapping out the beautiful moments they want to share in their lifetime together. Each stanza represents a different experience or adventure, from the simple joys of stargazing and first kisses to grander experiences like traveling to Antarctica, exploring Venice, or even ziplining through forests. The poem is not just a list of things to do, it's a celebration of love, intimacy, and the way these shared dreams create a deeper bond between two people.

This poem holds a special place in the storyline because it reflects the essence of planning a life together. It shows how a couple envisions their future, filled with unforgettable moments, each one a thread in the rich tapestry of their shared life. It's a testament to the idea that love isn't just about the present—it's about building a future filled with experiences, joy, and growth.

The real-life connection with the poem lies in the fact that many of the moments described in this list are taken from my personal love life with my girlfriend. These are experiences we've talked about, imagined, or even dreamt of doing together. For example, the references to stargazing, trips to places like Venice and Antarctica, and moments of laughter in the rain or on bike rides, are all things that hold meaning for us. Some of these dreams are already in the works, while others are simply aspirations that one day, we hope to bring to life.

In addition to the personal connections, the poem includes references to universal experiences that many couples can relate to, like holding hands for the first time, the excitement of a first proposal, or the simple pleasure of cooking together. The idea of creating a bucket list together, one that spans both small and grand dreams, becomes a metaphor for the commitment and love that fuels this journey. It's a reminder that life's beauty lies not just in the destination, but in the shared moments and the memories we create as we walk together. The poem shows that with love, the most ordinary things can become extraordinary, and every moment becomes part of a larger, beautiful story.

29. Lover Boy!

I am the man with the heart of an old song,
A lover who waits, where the shadows belong.
Like Ranjha, the poet, in a world so wide,
I'm lost in the longing that I cannot hide.
Imperfect, flawed, with a soul unrefined,
A tempest of passion, in a restless mind.
My heart, a wildfire, wild and unplanned,
Burns with the love that only you understand.
You are my sun, my stars, my moonlit skies,
The dream in my slumber, the light in my eyes.
Like Ash with Pikachu, so fierce and so true,
I am obsessed with you, I am devoted to you.
Every thought, every moment, all that I see,
Is colored by you, is wrapped in your melody.
You are the reason my heart skips and falls,
The echo that answers my love's deepest calls.
My imperfections, oh, they're plenty, my dear,
The storm in my chest, the trembling in fear.
I am a man of faults, with a temper so wild,
A boy who's both broken and easily riled.
Like a rough-edged diamond, raw and untamed,
I shout and I stumble, I'm never the same.
But in every flaw, in every wrong way,
Lies a love that's steadfast, that's here to stay.
I'm the type who would fight to the death,

For just one more moment, for your last breath.

In moments of anger, when shadows take flight,

I'm the one who breaks down in the dead of the night.

I'm the one who will chase you, wild-eyed and mad,

Trying to make up for the times that I've been bad.

Like Romeo's voice, desperate and bold,

I'll shout for your love, in stories retold.

But even in madness, there's poetry to be found,

A love that is fierce, that won't be bound.

My short temper, my rages, my stubborn pride,

They're nothing compared to the love I can't hide.

I'm the lover with roses that wilt in my hand,

The man who stands firm, who won't understand,

Why I am flawed, yet why I still care,

For you, my darling, for you, my prayer.

I may not be perfect, far from a knight,

With all of my battles, my wrongs and my fights.

But when it comes to you, when it comes to us,

I am a warrior, relentless and just.

Like Bruce Wayne in the night's dark embrace,

I'm both the hero and the man who'll face,

Every shadow, every fear, to keep you safe,

A love that's steadfast, no matter the stakes.

I am the lover, the maniac, the boy,

The one who will love you, your passionate, old-school lover boy.

Trivia For 'Lover Boy'

"Lover Boy" is a deeply personal poem, one that captures the essence of the lover in the storyline, someone who is imperfect, passionate, and relentlessly devoted. Unlike the other poems in the collection, which are primarily centered around the girlfriend and her emotions, "Lover Boy" focuses on the lover's perspective, giving us a glimpse into his heart, his flaws, and his undying devotion. This poem is a self-reflection of sorts, offering a raw and unflinching look at what it means to love intensely, even with all the imperfections that come with it.

The poem is, in many ways, a window into the type of lover I see myself as—a passionate, old-school romantic, someone whose love is both a strength and a flaw. It draws on literary and cultural references to illustrate the complexity of the lover's emotions, such as comparing the lover's unwavering devotion to that of Ranjha (from the famous Punjabi romance) and Romeo (from Romeo and Juliet). These references, along with mentions of Ash and Pikachu, Bruce Wayne, and other iconic figures, paint a picture of a lover who is both deeply committed and imperfect, fiercely protective yet vulnerable.

The lover described in the poem is someone who feels emotions with great intensity, his love is like a "wildfire," both consuming and exhilarating. There's a paradox in the way he expresses his love: he is a tempest of passion, yet a man who struggles with his own flaws, his anger, his fear, his imperfection. This duality is at the heart of the poem, reflecting the messy, chaotic nature of love itself. The lover is not a perfect knight in shining armor, but rather a man who fights his own demons while loving with all his might. This poem is special because it encapsulates the lover's perspective, making it a personal declaration of the love and passion I feel in my own heart. It's a tribute to the type of lover I strive to be—a passionate, old-school "lover boy," whose love, despite its flaws, is fierce, eternal, and unwavering.

30. Perfect You, Imperfect Me!

In a world full of stars, so brilliant and bright,

You, a constellation, caught my heart's sight.

I, a shadow, lost and unsure,

An imperfect being, a heart impure.

What could you have seen, in a man so flawed,

A soul so restless, so deeply raw?

While others shone with perfection's light,

I was the storm, in the dead of night.

Why did you choose me, when I was barely whole?

What secret spark did you see in my soul?

An immature heart, a mind so naive,

Yet you took a chance, you chose to believe.

A man who needed "servicing," as you called it,

Who fell short in every moment, and in it,

You were there, steadfast and true,

Never letting go, never bidding adieu.

I never deserved you, the greatest of all,

The one who would rise when I would fall.

You made me your hero, when I was a villain,

When I broke you, when I was unkind and chillin'.

You loved me like a mother, with patience so deep,

Even when I made you cry, even when you couldn't sleep.

You believed in me, when no one else did,

When I doubted myself, when I hid.

I remember the moments, each and every scar,
How you turned my pain to a guiding star.
From a fallen asteroid, lost in space,
You caught me, and with your grace,
You transformed me into a rising light,
A star reborn from the darkness of night.
You erased my bad habits, you made me strong,
Taught me to stand, taught me to belong.
How could someone so perfect choose someone so flawed?
Like the moon embracing the darkness, so raw.
Your greatness, unmatched, overpowers me,
A beauty, a soul, beyond what I can see.
You're the sun that banishes my storm,
The lighthouse that guides me back to form.
In your eyes, I see the truest art,
A love so pure, it stuns my heart.
And here I stand, with one question I can't dismiss,
Why did you choose me, in a world full of bliss?
What did you see in a man like me,
When there were so many who could make you free?
Your love has healed, transformed, and restored,
With you, I've found a life I can't afford,
A chance to be more, to rise from the floor,
But why, my love, did you choose me, and more?
I still wonder, with a heart full of grace,
What secret you hold in that luminous face.
You're perfect in a way that leaves me awestruck,
And I, an imperfect man, have been so lucky and struck.
You took a gamble, you chose this man,

And in your love, I found my plan.
And in moments when I was at my worst,
When my words were harsh, when my heart was cursed,
Did you never think, "I cannot bear this man"?
Did you ever feel, "This isn't part of the plan"?
Did you ever see the darkness in my soul,
And wonder if leaving would make you whole?
Did you look at me and see a demon in disguise,
And question your choice, with tears in your eyes?
Did you ever think of walking away,
Of letting go, of choosing another way?
But never you thought— "I am ashamed of my choice."
Your love was louder, your heart, your voice.
Through every storm, through every fight,
You stood by me, held me tight.
So I ask again, with every beat of my heart,
Why did you choose me, from the very start?

Trivia For 'Perfect You, Imperfect Me'

"Perfect You, Imperfect Me" is one of the most emotionally charged poems in this collection, delving deep into the heart of the lover's self-doubt and awe for his girlfriend. Written as a series of poignant questions from the lover to his partner, the poem explores the complexity of their relationship, with the lover wondering how and why she chose him, despite his many flaws. The poem is a heartfelt reflection of the lover's vulnerability, as he grapples with the notion that someone as perfect as her could love someone as imperfect as him.

The central theme of this poem is the lover's questioning of what it is that his girlfriend sees in him, an imperfect, often flawed man, when there are so many others out there who could potentially offer her a perfect love. He wonders if she saw something in him that no one else did, something worth believing in, despite his mistakes, flaws, and emotional storms. His insecurities are laid bare as he recalls the times he was distant, hurtful, or unkind, yet she chose to stay, to love, and to heal him.

The poem touches on the deep contrast between the lover's perception of his imperfections and the girlfriend's unwavering love. It reflects the emotional turbulence he experienced, feeling unworthy of her love, and yet being astonished by her patience and belief in him. The references to cosmic imagery, such as stars, the moon, and the sun, reflect the transformative power of her love, likening it to forces that bring light and guidance into his otherwise tumultuous world. He sees her as the sun that banishes his storms, a lighthouse that guides him back to his true self, and a figure of grace who transformed him into someone better.

On a personal level, the poem mirrors a deep, introspective thought that I, as the writer, often find myself reflecting on in my own relationship. It's a contemplation of why someone would choose to love a person who has made mistakes and who, at times, struggles to believe in their own worth. The questions posed in the poem are real-life questions I want to ask my girlfriend, questions about why, despite the heartaches and imperfections, she has chosen me, and what it is about me that she sees as worth loving.

"Perfect You, Imperfect Me" captures the raw, unfiltered emotions of self-doubt, love, and gratitude. It speaks to anyone who has ever felt unworthy of someone else's love, yet has been uplifted by that very love to become a better version of themselves. The poem beautifully conveys how love can be a transformative force, even when the person being loved feels far from perfect. It's a testament to the power of believing in each other, even when you can't always see the reasons why.

31. When Doubts Fall, Love Stands!

You say I won't handle your tantrums,

That I'll falter in the storm of your moods,

But love, you don't see the depth beneath my silence,

The oceans I'd sail just to make you smile.

You doubt if I'll see the queen you truly are,

Afraid your real self might fade in the shadow of my gaze.

But my heart beats only for you,

You are the moon, and I am the stars that orbit your light.

You fear I'll never treat you like the goddess you deserve,

That your laughter will fade in the weight of my rage.

But you don't know, love,

When you stop smiling, I too lose my joy.

If your eyes lose their sparkle, my soul will darken,

For your happiness is the light that fuels my heart.

When you're sad, the world crumbles beneath me,

And if the cause is me, I am lost forever.

You see my temporary rage and judge me for it,

But you don't know the lengths I would go

To turn every tear you shed into a pearl,

Every frustration into a reason to fight for you.

I would cry until my tears dried your thirst,

And when you're frustrated, I would be your punching bag,

Letting every blow be a lesson on how much I love you.

You think I might not be able to match your perfection,

But what you don't realize is you are my perfection.
I might never match your grace or maturity,
But, love, I will fight every day to deserve you.
You are the unicorn in my wildest dreams,
A beauty, rare and untouchable,
And I, the humble knight, can only hope to guard you forever.
When you feel lost, I will become your compass,
Guiding you with the strength of a thousand fireflies,
Lighting your path through every dark night.
When your heart is heavy, I will carry your burdens,
For my love for you is the wings of butterflies,
Gentle and infinite, lifting us both higher.
I dream of a life where your wishes are my commands,
Where every desire of yours is met before it's spoken,
Where your joy is my mission, my reason to exist.
I will build you a world, a universe, just for us,
Where we are the only two stars in the galaxy,
Shining brighter than all that came before.
But love, please believe me when I say,
Even my anger is a misguided attempt to protect you,
To shield you from the world that might hurt you,
I'm learning to control it,
But sometimes, I make a mess,
And in those moments, please know
I am only trying to be worthy of you,
Trying to be the man who can handle your fire
Without being burned by it.
When you say I can't handle your tantrums,
It tears my heart in ways I cannot describe.

Because, in truth, I would endure it all for you,

I would take every storm, every tempest,

Just to see you safe and happy.

For you are my Al Shifa, my healing,

In your smile, I find my cure,

In your embrace, I find my peace.

I would be the rain that falls,

Just to cleanse your soul of every sorrow.

And when you say I can't match your strength,

I bow before you, humbled,

For you are the queen, and I am your servant.

But never doubt that I will fight to the death

To protect you, to honor you,

To make your world shine as brightly

As you make mine.

So, love, when you doubt, remember this:

I will be your everything, your universe.

For you are the reason I breathe,

The rhythm of my heartbeat,

The kiss I long for in the morning,

The last thought on my mind at night.

I will never be perfect,

But I will always be yours,

Forever, endlessly,

And I will never be your regret.

Trivia For 'When Doubts Fall, Love Stands'

"When Doubts Fall, Love Stands" is one of the most heartfelt and emotionally intense poems in this collection, serving as a powerful response to doubts and insecurities in a relationship. This poem is written as a direct answer from the lover to his girlfriend, who, at times, fears that he may not be able to handle her moods and imperfections. The lover, in turn, reassures her of his unwavering commitment, love, and ability to handle whatever challenges come their way, no matter how difficult or trying. The poem is filled with deep emotional vulnerability and tenderness, as the lover acknowledges his flaws and shortcomings but insists that his love for her is stronger than any of the doubts that may arise.

The central theme of the poem revolves around the lover's desire to prove his devotion and ability to weather the storms of the relationship. His girlfriend, like many people in a relationship, sometimes questions if the partner can truly understand and embrace all of her—her flaws, her emotional outbursts, and her deeper fears. The poem begins by acknowledging her doubts, particularly about his ability to handle her "tantrums" or difficult moments. However, the lover passionately defends his readiness to face her struggles, believing that their love is strong enough to overcome any obstacle.

In the poem, the lover expresses his willingness to endure any hardship for her happiness, even comparing his willingness to be a "punching bag" for her frustrations, an image that symbolizes his deep love and understanding.

He highlights that even in moments of anger, his intentions are rooted in protecting her, and his emotional outbursts are not a reflection of weakness but an attempt to shield her from harm. The poem's recurring imagery of the moon and stars, as well as references to fireflies and butterflies, symbolize the lover's devotion, guidance, and strength, illustrating that his love for her is a constant source of light and support.

"When Doubts Fall, Love Stands" also explores themes of unconditional love and emotional resilience, demonstrating that love isn't about being perfect, but about being there for each other through the highs and lows.For anyone who has ever doubted their worth or questioned the strength of their relationship, this poem is a beautiful reminder that love, when genuine, can overcome doubts and fears. It emphasizes that true love isn't based on perfection, but on the willingness to face challenges together and to stand by one another through it all.

32. Masterpiece!

I searched for my masterpiece, a vision so rare,
Through moonlit nights and stardust air.
I looked in the heavens, where galaxies spun,
And in the shimmer of the first morning sun.
The stars whispered secrets, bright and deep,
But none could hold what my heart would keep.
I chased the meteor showers, a fleeting flight,
Wishing for a sign in their burning light.
I found beauty in butterflies, with wings so fine,
Their dance in the garden, a moment divine.
In fireflies at dusk, with their lanterns aglow,
I sought for that spark, that luminous show.
I captured the world through my poet's eyes,
In verses that soared, in heartfelt sighs.
Each word I wrote, each line I penned,
Was a quest, a search that would not end.
I wandered through forests, where the white tigers roam,
A symbol of power, of places unknown.
But even in their grace, their regal, fierce might,
There was nothing that captured my heart's light.
I took photographs of sunsets and dawns,
The whispers of nature, the breaking of morns.
Each frame a story, each shot a plea,
But still, none held what I failed to see.
It took time, it took years, it took knowing my soul,

To find the true piece that would make me whole.

I realized then, in that quiet space,

That my masterpiece was not a mere trace.

It was you, my love, my uncharted land,

Our love so vast, so perfectly planned.

The way we danced under the velvet sky,

The whispered words, the heartfelt goodbye.

Our story, an epic written in the stars,

With every laugh, every scar.

The way you lit up my dark, stormy seas,

And calmed the chaos, brought me to my knees.

A masterpiece born not in paint or rhyme,

But in moments shared, in the passage of time.

The constellations may have their tales to tell,

But ours is the story that outshines them all.

Our love, celestial, wild, and free,

The masterpiece I've been searching to see.

The painting in every sunrise, the song in the rain,

The poetry that soothes my heart's pain.

You are the canvas, the brush, the hue,

The masterpiece I've found, and it's you.

With every heartbeat, every glance, every sigh,

I know now, we were meant to be, you and I.

Trivia For 'Masterpiece'

"Masterpiece" is a profound and reflective poem that serves as one of the concluding pieces in the book "Celestial Love". This poem symbolizes the lover's journey of seeking perfection, beauty, and fulfillment throughout his life, only to realize that the true masterpiece he was searching for was always within reach: his love for her and the shared bond they have. The lover embarks on a quest for meaning, chasing fleeting moments of beauty in nature, the stars, and even the wild, but each discovery falls short of capturing his heart's deepest desire. It is only when he looks inward, to the love he shares with his partner, that he understands the true masterpiece is not a distant, unattainable vision, but the connection they've built together.

The poem begins with the lover searching for something "rare" and beautiful, symbolized by moonlit nights, galaxies, meteor showers, and fireflies. These elements, often seen as symbols of magic and wonder, represent his pursuit of beauty and meaning. However, each of these experiences ultimately leaves him longing for more, as none could truly touch the depth of his heart. As the poem progresses, the lover acknowledges the search for beauty through different forms, poetry, photography, nature, and the untamed wild. Yet, despite all these efforts, he realizes that none of these external wonders can compare to the love he has found with his partner. The "masterpiece" he was chasing all along was not a tangible creation or an external perfection, but the love that exists between them, a love that transcends time and space.

The poem's imagery is rich with symbolism: from the "butterflies" and "fireflies" representing fleeting beauty, to the "white tigers" symbolizing strength and majesty, each element contrasts with the ultimate realization that the lover's journey to find meaning was leading him to the love that already existed within their relationship. This realization reflects the theme of "Celestial Love", emphasizing that true beauty and perfection are not found in material pursuits but in the connection between two souls.

The poem beautifully connects the celestial imagery of the stars with the couple's personal story, asserting that their love is the one "story that outshines them all."This poem holds a special place in the collection as it is one of the final pieces that ties together the overarching themes of the book. "Celestial Love" is about searching for something greater than oneself, and in "Masterpiece", the lover has found it. The poem is not only a celebration of love but also a testament to the transformative power of love in helping one find purpose, meaning, and completion. In real-life context, this poem is deeply personal, as it reflects my journey of self-discovery and realization that true fulfillment comes not from external achievements or accolades, but from the love I share with my partner. It is a tribute to her, symbolizing that she is the one who completed my life's masterpiece—an eternal love that is, in essence, the most perfect creation he could ever dream of.

33. Love In Motion!

We boarded the train in separate ways,

Each of us bound for a journey of days.

The wheels hummed softly on tracks so wide,

But little did I know, the moment you'd arrive.

As the train swayed gently on its course,

I turned, and there you were, a dazzling force.

In your pink dress, you were Pegasus, pure,

An angel in motion, with beauty so sure.

Time seemed to still, the world stood still too,

As our eyes met and the universe knew.

Without a word, our souls intertwined,

In that moment, love was redefined.

We took our seats, so close, yet so far,

The train's hum a lullaby beneath the stars.

Your hand in mine, so soft, so warm,

As we shared stories in this fleeting storm.

You captured us in photos, so sweet,

A memory of love, a moment complete.

And then, my love, you fed me your heart,

A meal cooked with hands, a work of art.

Dinner was shared beneath the train's sway,

And as I tasted, my heart would stray

Into the wonders of you, so near,

And the love in your eyes I held so dear.

We turned to the window, the moon in view,

A soft silver glow in the night so true.

But then my love, my heart felt torn,

How could the moon be both here and worn?

With your gaze so gentle, so full of grace,

I leaned into your arms, lost in your face.

We watched a movie, the world outside blurred,

But nothing compared to the love I heard.

In your arms, the world was still,

The train moved on, but time was nil.

I gave your feet a tender touch,

A massage that spoke of love so much.

You held my head in your lap so soft,

And in your warmth, my thoughts took off.

I drifted to sleep in your loving care,

The most peaceful nap I've ever known was there.

Yet as I slept, I felt a pang of loss,

How could I waste these hours, the cost?

This journey so sweet, this time so divine,

How could I dream away this love so fine?

The moon, my love, soon faded from sight,

As the morning sun kissed the night.

And as the train rolled on, so true,

I knew the day was starting anew.

Twelve hours passed, yet felt like a life,

A journey of love, of peace, of strife.

The best train ride, the most sublime,

Together, my love, we transcended time.

We were stagnant in our berth, side by side,

But love was always in motion, far and wide.

For though the train would soon come to its end,
In our hearts, love would always transcend.

Trivia For 'Love In Motion'

"Love in Motion" is a heartfelt poem that captures the intimate and transformative experience of a lover and his girlfriend on their first train journey together. In this poem, the train becomes more than just a mode of transportation, it symbolizes the emotional and spiritual journey they take as a couple. The poem describes how, even in the small and simple moments shared between them, the lovers create a world of their own. From the gentle swaying of the train to the quiet hum of the wheels, every detail becomes infused with love and significance. The smallest acts, like holding hands, sharing stories, and enjoying a homemade meal together, elevate the journey into a beautiful memory that transcends time and place.

A particularly striking reference in the poem is the comparison of the girlfriend to Pegasus, the mythical winged horse of Greek mythology. This imagery captures her ethereal beauty and the sense of awe the lover feels in her presence. In a pink dress, she's described as an angel in motion, bringing a sense of magic and wonder to the journey, just as Pegasus would. This metaphor emphasizes the way the lover sees his girlfriend, not just as someone with whom he's sharing a moment, but as a transcendent figure who makes even the ordinary seem extraordinary.

The poem also emphasizes that the setting (a moving train) matters little when love is involved. The lovers don't need a grand, picturesque destination; their love and connection turn the train ride itself into a place of deep meaning. It's a reminder that sweet memories are not tied to specific places but are born from the moments we share with those we love. Despite the moving landscape outside the train, the lovers remain anchored in the present, cherishing every second of their time together. "Love in Motion" serves as a tribute to the idea that love is not confined to specific circumstances or grand gestures; instead, it lives in the simple, fleeting moments we create with the people we cherish. This poem is part of this collection because it explores the theme of how love, like the train ride, is always in motion, transforming ordinary moments into timeless memories.

34. The Paper Ring!

The lake glistened beneath the moon's soft gaze,
A silver path, a world set ablaze.
Around its edge, memories stood tall,
Our school benches, reminders of it all.
We sat there, hand in hand, lost in the past,
Whispers of a love that would forever last.
I reached for my book, pages worn and torn,
A story of us, where hearts were born.
You smiled as you read, eyes full of surprise,
Unraveling tales hidden deep in your eyes.
The words spoke of moments, laughter, and tears,
Of childhood days and innocent years.
"You wrote this?" you asked, your voice soft and true.
"Every line," I whispered, looking at you.
And as you read, the fireflies came,
A dance of lights, a beautiful flame.
The night held its breath, the world stood still,
As a butterfly emerged with grace and will.
In its delicate wings, a paper ring so bright,
It hovered, gliding in the gentle night.
It landed in my hands, fragile and sweet,
A symbol of love, our hearts to meet.
Your eyes widened as I kneeled by the lake,
Our cat sat nearby, a witness to the stake.
The stars above twinkled, a cosmic shower,

A shower of love, an endless power.

A unicorn emerged from the moon's soft glow,

Its mane like silver, its eyes pure and slow.

With a nod and a touch, it beckoned us near,

We climbed on, hearts free of any fear.

Butterflies flew, forming a celestial guard,

As we soared, hearts racing, with love so hard.

The moon embraced us, cool and bright,

We stood on its surface, bathed in its light.

Our love, a pulse, a single, shared beat,

As you turned to me, a moment so sweet.

Your lips found mine in a kiss so deep,

A promise made, a secret to keep.

The paper ring gleamed, a symbol so pure,

A love that time and space couldn't obscure.

On the moon, where dreams come to play,

We held each other, night turning to day.

The book still lay, open on the bench,

Pages turning, each word a love-stretched quench.

The wind flipped to the last page, revealing a note,

A memory, a truth, a love we wrote.

"Two young kids exchanged red roses once,

Never thought they'd create a love so intense.

The boy would write poetries about her,

Little did they know, their love would stir

A world beyond, a story so bright,

Branded as 'celestial love,' an eternal light."

In that moment, with stars that still fell,

A love story told, a fairytale to tell.

We kissed, our souls as one, so close,
The paper ring, a vow that forever chose.
And as we stood on the moon, hearts intertwined,
I knew with you, I'd always find my home, my sign.

Trivia For 'The Paper Ring'

"The Paper Ring" serves as part of the grand, emotional climaxes of the book "Celestial Love", marking a transformative moment in the relationship between the lover and his girlfriend. This poem is not only a creative proposal but also an acknowledgment of the playful and sincere dynamics between the two. It brings together the themes of love, memory, and the shared dreams that have defined their connection.

The poem begins with a nostalgic scene by a shimmering lake where the couple sits, reflecting on the past. The lover's act of sharing a written book about their story symbolizes the depth of his affection for her, a love that has grown over time, through laughter, tears, and moments both big and small. The magical atmosphere, filled with fireflies and the whimsical imagery of a butterfly with a paper ring, creates the perfect backdrop for a proposal. The use of the paper ring in this poem is deeply significant, not only because it is an element of the proposal but also because it is a playful nod to real-life interactions between the poet and his girlfriend.

In real life, I frequently teased my girlfriend about proposing with a paper ring, while she would jokingly express her desire for a diamond ring. This poem takes that playful teasing and elevates it to an extraordinary moment, where the lover presents the "paper ring" in a grand, fantastical manner, surrounded by the moon, stars, and a unicorn, illustrating just how special and irreplaceable she is to him, even if the proposal isn't what society might consider traditional. The paper ring is symbolic of his genuine affection and the pure, unpretentious love they share.

The concluding lines, which feature the lover's wish for her acceptance of the paper ring, are a touching and sincere attempt to make a public, yet intimate, declaration of love. By including this in the book, the lover opens his heart in front of the world, leaving behind a testament of love that is both playful and deeply sincere. "The Paper Ring" is not just a proposal; it is an embodiment of their shared journey, a romantic gesture rooted in humor, creativity, and, above all, a love that is vast and unyielding. The lover's hope that she will accept the paper ring is not just a wish for a future together, but a celebration of the simple yet profound truth that their love, like the stars, is eternal.

35. The Cat We Loved!

We found you one summer evening,

a flicker of fur beneath the trees,

Your emerald eyes, wide, unblinking,a secret only you could keep.

We named you Hazel, soft as dawn,

And you curled in the crook of our arms as the world turned golden with heat,

Summer air thick with the scent of grass

and the murmur of distant frogs.

You were the first thing I held that made me believe in magic,

Your purring, a lullaby that wove the threads of our hearts together.

I remember you watching us, your little paws tracing the edges of our world, night falling,

The sky filled with fireflies dancing in the velvet dark.

Winter came, quiet and cold,but you never seemed to mind.

Your warm body curled against my side as snow blanketed the earth in soft silence.

We'd wake to mornings bright with frost,and you, with your little nose pressed against the glass,

Would watch the world and the snowflakes fall in slow motion.

A snail's slow crawl across the windowsill was your only distraction in those mornings,

And you'd bat it away with soft paws,as if teasing the world to stop for you.

We'd chase the stars together on those clear nights,dreams of endless roads in the curve of your tail.

You'd perch on the windowsill, a queen surveying her kingdom,

While we whispered to the moon, each promise we made to you,

Carried on the back of a meteor,a streak of light and hope across the sky.

Through the spring rains, you walked beside us in the wet grass,

Your fur dotted with droplets,paws leaving soft marks in the mud.

I remember how we laughed, your little mew rising over the sound

Of thunder cracking in the distance,and how we ran, hand in hand,

To escape the storm while you stayed,bold, a shadow chasing butterflies in the deluge.

But time is a cruel thing.

And summer turned to fall,leaves danced in colors,

But your steps began to slow, your eyes dimmed like a fading star whose light had nowhere left to go.

The day you stopped chasing frogs was the day we knew.

The quiet in your purr, the thinness in your coat,

A silence that spread between us like the first frost on the ground.

We took you to the vet, the sterile smell of antiseptic

A stark contrast to the smell of rain that used to cling to your fur.

The doctor's face was a mask of sorrow,

And all we could do was hold you close and promise you we'd never let you go.

You slept on our laps that night, the last night you were still Hazel,

Your body growing weaker by the hour,

Your little breath a soft sigh against the weight of our hands.

The morning came, and the sun rose,

a pale light spilling through the window where you once sat, eyes wide, watching the world.

But now, it was just us, holding the space where you had been,

The silence so loud in the room that we could hear the echoes of every memory you gave us.
And when you left, it felt as though the sky itself had wept.
The moon, a ghost of its former self, hid behind clouds that would never part again.
The stars blinked out one by one, the fireflies extinguished, and the world seemed to grow dim.
We buried you beneath the old oak tree, where we first found you,
Beneath the roots that spread like arms and the grass that would never forget the paw prints you left behind.
We whispered our goodbyes, and though you couldn't hear us,
I swear you felt it, the weight of all the love we gave you and the grief that would stay
in the hollow of our hearts forever.
And now, the nights feel colder, the mornings a little too quiet.
But sometimes, just before the dawn, I can feel you still,
Your soft paws padding through the grass,
Your tail brushing against the wind, your eyes, still wide, still watching.
In every summer, in every rain, in every star that falls from the sky,
You'll live on in the echoes of the love you gave us and the love we could never repay.

Trivia For 'The Cat We Loved'

"The Cat We Loved" is one of the most emotionally charged poems in this collection, and for good reason. It reflects the deep emotional bond between two people and the pet they find, care for, and love as if it were their own child. The poem is a tribute not only to the beloved cat, Hazel, but also to the impact pets can have on relationships. In the poem, I wanted to show how a pet especially one as special as Hazel can strengthen the love between two people, providing emotional stability and a sense of shared joy. The simple, everyday moments with Hazel, from watching her play in the rain to curling up with her during winter, became a beautiful extension of our love. It was in these moments that we truly understood how a pet can shape and deepen the bond between two people.

I chose to write about a cat because both my girlfriend and I have always shared a love for cats. I chose the name Hazel because I always dreamed of giving this name to a cat I would someday have. In this poem, she wasn't just a pet to them; she became part of their world, a symbol of everything they had built together. Hazel brought a certain magic to their lives, her purring was a lullaby that soothed their hearts, and her presence, even in silence, made everything feel complete. However, like all good things, their time with Hazel was finite. The day they had to say goodbye to her was one of the hardest moments, and I poured that grief into this poem. Her death became a symbol of separation, not just of losing her, but also a reflection of the inevitable separations we face in life. Despite that, Hazel's memory remains with them. It's through the tears and the quiet moments that they feel her still, her paws padding through the grass, her eyes still watching over them.

This poem is a tribute to that loss, but it's also a celebration of how much pets can enrich our lives. They teach us how to love more deeply, how to share our hearts, and how to find beauty in even the smallest moments. The impact Hazel had on them, especially on heir relationship, is something we should forever carry with ourselves. Even though she's gone, she'll live on in the love they shared, and in the quiet memories that will always echo in their hearts.

36. Northern Lights!

Beneath the cosmic velvet sky, where whispers of the stars entwine,

The northern lights, like liquid dreams, across the heavens' edge, they shine.

Once, as children, we dared to dream, our hearts alight with whispered songs,

Of auroras dancing in the night, where our love would find its home.

Now, here we stand, beneath this glow, where fireflies kiss the air,

Their wings alive in trembling light, while we, as one, embrace what's rare.

The world has vanished in the glow of this electric, starry sea,

And all that matters in this world, my love, is you and me.

Rest your lips upon my own, let them taste the fire,

As we exchange our souls, my dear, and kindle our desire.

For this is more than just a kiss, it's where two hearts collide,

In every touch, in every breath, where our spirits do not hide.

Like reindeer moving through the snow, their shadows soft and deep,

We walk in silence, lost in love, where time forgets to keep.

The icefall murmurs, carved by time, a symphony of frozen tears,

Yet in your arms, my darling love, I leave behind my fears.

We once imagined, side by side, to chase the aurora's mystic thread,

To witness light beyond the world, to see what others said.

But now, here, in this moment bright, where the night begins to weave,

We dance beneath the northern glow, with hearts that never grieve.

An aurora butterfly, aglow, it flutters softly in our world,

Wings spun of light and ancient dreams, in time's embrace unfurled.
With every twist and every turn, our hearts like fireflies ignite,
Dancing in the silence of the sky, beneath the cosmic light.
The heavens bow before our steps, as we glide in perfect tune,
Our bodies speak a language clear, beneath the silver moon.
This dance is ours, and ours alone, as time stands still, it seems,
The beauty of the cosmos pales, beside the love in our dreams.
The world is vast, yet here we are, two souls as bright as flame,
Caught in a fire only we know, where nothing's ever the same.
Each breath we take is endless joy, each word a whispered prayer,
In the stillness of the night, my love, there's magic in the air.
Oh, what could be more beautiful than this moment, rich and true,
Where every light within the sky reflects the love I have for you?
And though the northern lights may fade, and fireflies flicker out,
Our love will burn forever bright, with no shadow, no doubt.
So, as you gaze upon the lights, so wondrous in their glow,
Know that in your eyes, my love, a greater light does show.
Your eyes were looking at those lights, but my eyes saw the brighter
lights,
That were your eyes.

Trivia For 'Northern Lights'

"Northern Lights" is a poetic tribute to a long-held dream shared between two lovers, their wish to witness the ethereal beauty of the aurora borealis. This poem was inspired by a personal vision of an extraordinary romance unfolding under the glowing lights of the northern sky. The idea of this dream coming true, set against the backdrop of nature's most mesmerizing spectacle, became the perfect setting to explore the deep, magical connection between the lovers.

In the poem, the lover and his girlfriend find themselves beneath the cosmic velvet sky, surrounded by the shimmering northern lights. The vivid imagery of reindeer moving through snow, fireflies dancing in the air, and the creation of an "Aurora Butterfly" symbolize the rare beauty of their moment together. The "Aurora Butterfly" is a personal, imaginative creation that first appeared in this poem, symbolizing the delicate and fleeting nature of both the auroras and their love interwoven with light, dreams, and time.

The poem goes beyond a simple description of the auroras; it captures the essence of a deeper connection between the two people, whose love transcends the natural wonders surrounding them. While the northern lights are a stunning visual spectacle, the poem subtly reveals the lover's belief that the true beauty lies in his girlfriend's eyes. In the last line, he confesses that while she was enchanted by the lights above, it was her eyes that truly outshone everything. This moment serves as a testament to his devotion, highlighting how his love for her is greater than the grandeur of nature itself.

Though "Northern Lights" was not originally part of this collection, its inclusion felt right after a serendipitous moment when I saw something related to the auroras. It perfectly aligns with the overall theme of the book, cosmic, starry landscapes, and the idea that true love is written in the stars. In this poem, the celestial beauty of the northern lights becomes the perfect metaphor for the lovers' bond, where every light in the sky reflects the depth of their affection and their shared, timeless connection. It serves as both an ode to the wonder of the cosmos and a celebration of a love that shines brighter than any star.

37. You Are The Blue In My Painting!

Since I was a child, the canvas whispered to me,

Of worlds waiting to be painted, of skies yearning to be free.

I brushed the colors, vivid and wild,

But a void remained an emptiness in my heart,

For the sky had no blue, no whisper of the moon,

And I, a desperate artist, was left incomplete.

You see, the blue I sought was not in the earth,

Not in the oceans, or the rivers, or the dawn,

It was hidden, secret, cradled in the heart of the moon.

And so I went, where no soul dared to tread,

To the pale silver stone, where time and silence bled.

There, I found it, a piece of that pale blue,

A glimmer so rare, it outshone even the Kohinoor's hue.

A stone that held the essence of the night sky,

A treasure whispered of in lullabies.

It pulsed with light, with a soft, ethereal glow,

The blue of the heavens, the kind you only know

When you stare up long enough to see the stars sigh.

I brought it back, my heart heavy with joy,

But when I gave it to you, my love, it was not for my painting, you
thought it was for you.

Your eyes, brighter than the stone, shone with delight,

Like the first rays of dawn kissing the night goodbye.

You thought it was for you, and I,

I watched the tears of joy, like pearls in the rain,

Falling from your eyes,

A silent symphony, a melody that echoed

The love that had lived between us for all time.

I could never tell you it wasn't for you,

But as I saw you smile, my heart twisted in truth,

For what good is a painting without the essence of you?

Your joy, your tears, the sparkle in your gaze,

They were the colors I needed, the final phrase.

So, I mixed the tears with the blue from the stone,

Blended them with the softness of my own.

A new color emerged more beautiful than the rainbow,

A color that held both sorrow and love in its flow.

It was not just blue, not just the moonlight's glow,

It was the color of us, of sacrifice and dreams,

Of love too pure for the world to hold.

And with it, my painting was complete,

The sky was no longer empty,

And I was no longer incomplete.

You, my love,

You are the blue in my painting,

The color that made the world whole,

The sky, the stone, the butterfly's flight,

You are the answer, the sacrifice, the light.

Trivia For 'You Are The Blue In My Painting'

"You Are Blue in My Painting" is a unique and deeply symbolic poem that blends fantasy with the tender realities of love and sacrifice. The poem shows the lover who has been creating a painting for years, but it remains incomplete without one essential color, the blue that is meant to fill the sky. After searching the earth and finding no trace of this elusive hue, the lover ventures to the moon, where he discovers a rare blue stone, glowing with the light of the heavens. When he brings it back, however, he doesn't tell his girlfriend that the stone is not for her, and she, mistaking it as a gift for herself, reacts with tears of joy. In that moment, the lover realizes that the essence of his creation is not the stone or the color itself, but the emotions shared with his partner.

This poem is a metaphor for the sacrifices we make in relationships, sacrifices that are often imperceptible but deeply meaningful. The lover could have kept the blue stone for his painting, but he chose to give it to his girlfriend, embodying the idea that sometimes our personal goals or ambitions must be set aside in order to nurture love and grow together. The blue in the painting, originally sought as an element for artistic expression, ultimately becomes a symbol of the shared love and emotions between the two, blending his artistic vision with the genuine joy and tears of his partner.

The message in this poem is that love often requires selflessness. To grow as a couple, sometimes we must give up our personal desires, knowing that the sacrifices we make will help complete the picture of our shared life. The "blue" in the lover's painting becomes a symbol of love itself, a color not found in the world until it's created through their bond. This act of giving, of making a painting whole with the joy of his partner, speaks to the essence of true love, where the blending of two hearts makes something far greater than either could have achieved alone. Ultimately, "You Are Blue in My Painting" is a meditation on the transformative power of love, how two individuals, through their sacrifices and shared experiences, can create a masterpiece together, making the world feel complete.

38. Shiuli!

In October's breath, a quiet spell,
The earth hums softly, where shadows dwell,
Beneath the sky's wide, velvet sweep,
The night, like secrets, softly speaks.
Shiuli blooms in twilight's kiss,
Each petal born from autumn's bliss,
A fragrant whisper on the air,
A symbol of the love we share.
We are like these flowers, my dear,
In moments when the world feels near,
And yet so far, we fall and rise,
But through it all, we reach the skies.
For every tear that leaves the eye,
A deeper root begins to lie,
We are like Shiuli, brave and true,
Born from the dark, but bathed in dew.
The fall is gentle, sweet and kind,
For in each drop, new strength we find.
And though the night may wear us thin,
We rise again, where love begins.
Your hand in mine, we face the dawn,
No sorrow can keep us withdrawn.
For love, like flowers, finds its way,
Through autumn's dusk, into the day.

The Shiuli falls, its petals wane,
But in the loss, there is no pain.
For love, my love, is ever bright,
A bloom that rises from the night.
The Shiuli's scent, a balm so sweet,
It fills the air where hearts first meet.
A fragrance soft, like whispered dreams,
That lingers in the quiet streams.
In every petal's fleeting grace,
I find the warmth of your embrace.
It tells of love that gently grows,
A memory that forever flows.
So let the petals fall, my dear,
For in our hearts, we hold no fear.
We are the dawn, the sky, the rain,
Forever blooming through the pain.
And though the seasons come and go,
Our love will bloom, as pure as snow.
The Shiuli falls, but love will stand,
Two hearts, forever hand in hand.

Trivia For 'Shiuli'

"Shiuli" is a deeply personal poem that carries a profound message about love, resilience, and the beauty found in life's inevitable cycles of joy and sorrow. While Shiuli, or the "Night Jasmine," is traditionally seen as a symbol of sadness and mourning due to its association with autumn and its fleeting bloom, I have chosen to present it in a more positive light. To me, Shiuli represents the strength that comes from embracing the full spectrum of emotions, joy, sorrow, and everything in between. Its delicate fragrance, often considered melancholic, becomes in this poem a symbol of love's quiet, enduring beauty.

The inspiration for this poem stems from my own personal connection with Shiuli, which is my favorite flower. I've also been influenced by its prominent role in the movie "October", a film that beautifully portrays the complexity of true love. The movie's exploration of love through pain and loss resonated deeply with me, and the Shiuli, as a motif in the film, served as a perfect metaphor for how love can bloom even in the most difficult of times.

In "Shiuli," I have used the flower as a metaphor for a relationship that falls and rises, much like the petals of the flower that bloom and fall with the seasons. This poem illustrates the powerful message that, even when life is challenging, love like the Shiuli can rise again, more beautiful and resilient than before. It's a reminder that, despite the storms we face, we always have the chance to start anew, together. Through this, the Shiuli becomes an emblem of love's unbreakable bond, teaching us that we must fall together and rise together, no matter what the world may throw our way. This poem, placed at a pivotal moment in the collection, signals a turning point a departure from sorrow into strength, and ultimately, a reaffirmation of love that persists through all seasons. Shiuli, in my vision, becomes not a symbol of sadness but of renewal, growth, and the unshakeable bond between two souls. Also, signalling the unexpected climax of this storyline.

39. The Fallen Star!

Once, we stargazed like dreamers,
You beside me, wrapped in the glow of the moon,
The universe sprawled at our feet,
As we traced constellations in the vast unknown,
We were fireflies in the dark,
Flickering bright in the coldness of time,
Until our hearts beat in the same rhythm,
Filling the void between us with every whispered promise.
I remember how you laughed,
The way the stars seemed to pause,
As if they too listened to the story we built,
Each chapter was a flame,
A butterfly's flight across a midnight sky.
The first time I wrote your name in verse,
My pen trembled, the ink a love letter to the cosmos,
But you,
You read it like it was our first kiss,
A spark that set the universe alight.
Do you remember our first date?
We stood beneath the silver moon,
The world spinning,
But we stayed still,
Two hearts bound by invisible threads.
And our first train journey,
The rhythm of the tracks,

Your hand in mine like a sacred vow.

Every mile was a memory,

Every glance a galaxy we discovered together.

But now, my love,

I can see you struggling,

As I drift further away,

Like a star lost in the dark,

Forgotten in the vastness of time and space.

I forget our first hug,

The warmth of your arms

That made the coldest nights feel like spring.

I forget the way you smiled,

As if the world was made only for us,

The rarest Suicune in a world full of fleeting moments.

I try, you know,

I try to hold on,

But the memories slip through my fingers,

Like sand in the wind,

And I can't find the path back.

Your voice echoes in my ears,

A lighthouse in the fog,

Trying to guide me to the shores of our past.

You remind me of the stars we promised to chase,

Of the adventures we wrote on our bucket list,

Of our holiday in Venice,

Where the canals were our love,

And Antarctica, where the cold was nothing

But a reason to hold you closer.

But no matter how hard you try,

I am slipping away,
Like a comet fading into the abyss.
Alzheimer's, a thief in the night,
Stealing fragments of who we were,
Taking pieces of me,
While you fight to hold onto us,
To the love we shared,
As my mind crumbles like old paper,
Pages turning to blank.
And yet, in your eyes,
I see it,
That celestial love,
The love that defies time and space,
The love that once belonged to me,
And now, in your tears,
I see it still burning.
So here, my dear, in this moment,
You kiss my forehead,
And I am a child again,
Lost in your arms,
And you whisper softly,
"Now it's my turn.
To love you as you did to me,
From a distance,
A love unspoken,
A one-sided love that now fills the space between us.
I will be your Bruce Wayne,
And you, my Gotham,
I will fight for you in the shadows,

Even if the world forgets.

And if the stars don't remember our names,

I will kiss you,

And love you still,

In the silence of the cosmos,

For as long as the universe allows.

So let me be your one-sided lover now,

Your heart's quiet secret,

As you were once mine.

I'll be your whisper in the wind,

Your starlight, your endless flame,

And you, my cute little girl,

Will be the love that never fades."

Trivia For 'The Fallen Star'

"The Fallen Star" serves as the powerful climax to this collection, offering a poignant and unexpected conclusion. Throughout the book, the theme of love has evolved from fleeting, youthful infatuations to deep, soul-connecting devotion. However, the ending of this collection veers away from the conventional, offering an emotional and profound message: true love is not about constant happiness or perfection, but about being present for each other through the darkest of times. In this final poem, the concept of "celestial love" takes center stage, suggesting a love that transcends the bounds of time, memory, and even life itself.

The poem's narrative revolves around a couple facing the heartbreaking progression of Alzheimer's disease. As the boyfriend slowly loses his memories, the girlfriend remains steadfast in her devotion. The use of Alzheimer's is not incidental; the poet drew inspiration from reading about the condition and sought to explore the idea of love amidst inevitable loss. The devastating effects of memory loss symbolize the finality of life, yet within this decay, the poem illuminates a love that remains constant, pure and unshakable despite the ravages of time and illness.

One of the most emotionally charged references in this poem is the mention of "Bruce Wayne" (the Batman) who, despite Gotham's rejection and the personal costs of his crusade, chooses to stay and fight for the city. This mirrors the girlfriend's unwavering commitment to her boyfriend even as he forgets their shared memories. The comparison between Bruce Wayne's love for Gotham and the girlfriend's love for her partner elevates their bond to something extraordinary. Even as her boyfriend's mind crumbles, she chooses to stay, embodying the true meaning of "celestial love." This love is not bound by physical presence or recognition, but by a deep, eternal connection that persists beyond the universe itself.

Another striking image in the poem is the reference to "Suicune", a rare and elusive Pokémon, symbolizing the uniqueness and purity of their love. In a full circle of emotional depth, "The Fallen Star" begins with the lover as the one-sided figure, his passion and longing driving the narrative as he yearns for the affection of his partner. The journey through the collection maps his transformation from an eager, passionate soul to one who learns the complexities and nuances of love. But in the climax, this role is reversed. Now, it is the girlfriend who becomes the one-sided lover, silently bearing the weight of his fading memories and the slow unraveling of their shared past. While the lover's passion was evident from the start, the ending reveals the intensity of the girlfriend's love, which has grown even more profound and enduring. Her love is now the quiet, selfless force that holds them both together, even as his mind drifts further away. Where the lover once held the torch, now she does, embodying a passion that is not marked by grand gestures but by an unwavering commitment to love, despite the inevitable loss. This reversal of roles highlights the depth of true love: it evolves, adapts, and endures, growing stronger even when faced with the greatest of challenges.

In the closing lines, the girlfriend's declaration, "Now it's my turn. To love you as you did to me... I'll be your whisper in the wind, Your starlight, your endless flame..." brings the poem to a heart-wrenching and beautiful close. It's here that the girlfriend fully embodies the role of the selfless lover, echoing the sentiment that love, when true, doesn't demand to be remembered or reciprocated in the same way. Instead, it exists beyond the physical realm, echoing through the quiet moments, the whispers of the wind, and the silent strength of a devotion that doesn't falter.

Ultimately, "The Fallen Star" encapsulates the book's central message: Love, in its purest form, is not something that fades with time or circumstances. It is the force that carries us through the worst of what life can bring. Even when the stars fall, even when nothing is left, love is the one weapon we have that endures. In this way, the poem and the collection as a whole ends not with despair, but with an enduring, celestial love that continues to shine in the darkest of nights.

40. Celestial Love!

It began as a spark,
A whisper beneath the moon's glow,
A flicker, a flutter, a dream untouched,
Two souls crossing paths in the vastness of time.
Like butterflies caught in the breath of the universe,
We danced on the winds of Confession,
Your eyes the stars, my heart the flame,
A love ignited from nothing,
Yet destined to burn beyond worlds.
You and I, You, Me, and Rain,
The rhythm of our love traced in the droplets,
A heartbeat beating in tune with the cosmos,
Beyond Heartache, we found our way,
Each pulse a promise, each touch a galaxy.
In the silence of the night, we whispered
Of Romance So Sweet,
And the stories we wrote in the stars,
Love Written in Stars,
A constellation of us,
Forever bound in this endless sky.
Time did not ask permission,
But we stood still,
Infinity Forever,
Like fireflies in the dark,
Flickering bright against the pull of night's gravity.

Through When Doubts Fall, Love Stands,
We held each other steady,
Two souls anchored by an invisible thread,
Unseen yet unbroken.
A Masterpiece of passion and patience,
We were each other's northern lights,
Radiating color across the endless night,
Love in motion,
A journey that never stopped,
Never wavered,
Always, always reaching for something greater.
And now, as I fade like a Fallen Star,
You become the light that guides me through the dark,
A love that was always there,
In every universe,
In every parallel sky.
Like a unicorn born from stardust,
Our love transcends beyond every boundary,
A love beyond the world's limits,
Beyond even the cosmos,
A love that defies all time and space.
Through every Us in Every Universe,
Through every Heartbeat lost and found,
Through every Fallen Star and Northern Light,
We are, we always were,
Celestial, forevermore.

Trivia For 'Celestial Love'

"Celestial Love" is the title poem of the collection, serving as both the culmination and the thematic essence of the entire book. While it is not part of the storyline, it ties together the various threads explored throughout the poems, acting as a bridge that connects all the themes-love, time, loss, and devotion. This poem encapsulates the core message of the book: love that transcends boundaries, defies the limits of time and space, and persists even in the face of the greatest challenges.

The poem opens with a subtle beginning, reflecting the spark of love that grows over time into something extraordinary and eternal. Through references to other poems in the collection, such as Confession, You, Me, and Rain, Beyond Heartache, Love Written in Stars, Infinity Forever, and When Doubts Fall, Love Stands, Celestial Love weaves the emotional journey of the lovers, from the spark of connection to a love that exists beyond physical realms. These poems collectively create the backdrop for this final reflection, highlighting the transcendence of love as it evolves from a fleeting moment to something cosmic.

One of the poem's central motifs is the imagery of the cosmos, unicorns, northern lights, fireflies, and the stars. These elements symbolize the rare and ethereal nature of the love shared by the lovers, one that continues even as time and memory fade. The reference to Fallen Star suggests that even in moments of loss or darkness, the light of love persists, guiding the lovers through the unknown. The phrase Love in Motion evokes the idea of a journey that never ends, a movement that transcends the limitations of space and time.

Ultimately, "Celestial Love" serves as the book's thematic crux: a love that, like the stars, exists beyond the realm of human understanding, lighting the way through both the bright and dark moments of life. It leaves the reader with the powerful message that true love, no matter the circumstances, is eternal, unyielding, and always, celestial, forever burning bright, even in the silence of the cosmos. This final poem brings the collection full circle, wrapping the themes of passion, loss, and eternal connection into a profound, otherworldly declaration of love.

Outro

As the final page of "Celestial Love" turns, the journey of this extraordinary love story comes to an end, but the echoes of the words, the emotions, and the memories linger on, forever etched in the heart. This book, born from the depths of my soul, tells the tale of a one-sided lover who became everything for the person he loved. A journey from doubt to promise, from yearning to forever, this collection of poems has been my way of sharing the love I hold for the one who transformed my world.

Each verse, each line, was written with you in mind, my love. Every word reflects the reality of our bond, how you brought color to my life and taught me what it means to love without limits. From the firefly's gentle whisper to the constellations' timeless glow, this book is a celebration of "us", a love story that is written not just in words, but in every heartbeat, every glance, and every shared moment.

As this book closes, remember that true love is a journey that never truly ends. It is written in the stars, carried through time and space, and felt in every breath. And though the chapters of this book have come to a close, the love we share continues to evolve, just like the stars, endless, bright, and ever-shining.

This book is the culmination of a dream, a confession, a promise, and the truest love I could ever hope to give. So, as you close the cover, know that my words will always be here, waiting for you, just as my love will.

Thank you for being the reason I believed in love, for inspiring every line, every page, and for filling my life with a story that will forever be more extraordinary than I ever imagined. And as we continue this journey together, side by side, my heart will always write for you.

Poet's Desk

Mohammad Yusuf, the author of "Celestial Love", is a passionate poet and storyteller who writes from the heart. With a keen eye for the world around him, he finds inspiration in even the smallest moments of life, weaving them into beautiful tales and poems. A B.Com graduate from Delhi University and a CA aspirant with a focus on taxation and auditing, Mohammad's life reflects a unique blend of two worlds—one of numbers and spreadsheets, and another of words and emotions.

Though "Celestial Love" marks his debut in the world of publishing, this book wasn't initially meant to be his first. In fact, he has another work still in progress. However, the poems in "Celestial Love" poured out naturally, each one inspired by the love he has for his girlfriend. The emotions were raw, true, and pure, and they formed the foundation for this extraordinary love story told through 40 poems.

Mohammad's journey as a writer began during his school days, when he would write poems in his free time. Back then, he never imagined that one day he would publish a book. Today, he feels blessed and grateful to have come this far. First and foremost, he thanks Allah, the Almighty, for guiding him throughout this journey. He also expresses his heartfelt gratitude to his family for their unwavering support. But most importantly, he dedicates this book to the love of his life, his girlfriend, who has always been the driving force behind his writing.

It has always been a dream of hers for Mohammad to publish his debut book, and this is his way of fulfilling that wish. She may have thought that he had given up on writing, but with "Celestial Love", he hopes to surprise her in the most beautiful way. Mohammad is deeply grateful to his readers, whose support and encouragement have made this journey possible.

"Celestial Love" is a heartfelt gift, an ode to the love of his life, and now, it is yours, deep from his heart.

Thank You For Reading !

If you have any feedback or any message for the author,

Connect with him: Instagram @aurora._.butterfly

Email: aurorabutterflyyyyy@gmail.com

"In the Last Birthday, You just asked for a poem
But Now I've burnt pages with my fiery tone.
You used to flex, I wrote poetries for you,
Now flex, I wrote a book for you, forever true"
-Mohammad Yusuf